KIDS' BOOK OF
FIGURE SKATING

D1258464

KIDS' BOOK OF
FIGURE SKATING

Rikki Samuels

Illustrations by Dennis Wunderlin

CITADEL PRESS
Kensington Publishing Corp.
www.kensingtonbooks.com

CITADEL PRESS BOOKS are published by

Kensington Publishing Corp.
850 Third Avenue
New York, NY 10022

Copyright © 2004 Rikki Samuels

All Kensington titles, imprints, and distributed lines are available at
special quantity discounts for bulk purchases for sales promotions,
premiums, fund-raising, educational, or institutional use. Special book
excerpts or customized printings can also be created to fit specific needs.
For details, write or phone the office of the Kensington special sales
manager: Kensington Publishing Corp., 850 Third Avenue, New York,
NY 10022, attn: Special Sales Department; phone 1-800-221-2647.

CITADEL PRESS and the Citadel logo are Reg. U.S. Pat. & TM Off.

First printing: November 2004

10 9 8 7 6 5 4 3 2 1

Printed in the United States of America

Library of Congress Control Number: 2004106176

ISBN 0-8065-2601-7

CONTENTS

PART THREE: FOR SERIOUS SKATERS   *159*

9. I Think I Have Talent—What's Next?   161

Keeping Things in Perspective • How to Save
Money and Time • Choosing a Coach • What To
Expect from a Coach • What Your Coach Expects
from You • How To Get the Most from Your
Lessons • The Role of Your Parents • Boots:
Custom-Made vs. Store-Bought • Mounting and
Sharpening of Blades

PART FOUR: FOR FANS OF SKATING   *171*

10. How to Be an Informed Fan   173

Skating Shows at Your Local Arena • Live
Competitions

11. I Don't Skate, but I Want to Be Involved   177

Help Wanted: Volunteers • Designing Skating
Costumes • Happy Skating!

LIST OF ILLUSTRATIONS

ACKNOWLEDGMENTS

Behind every book are so many helpers, authorities, encouragers, and talents. All were very important to me, and I want to thank them.

Michaela Hamilton and Ann LaFarge, my editorial geniuses, who had an idea and made it happen. Joan Tennant and Miles Lott, my computer consultants. All my coaches and students, who never stop teaching me. Dennis Wunderlin, my skating student and illustrator. Candi Harper, a friend whose encouragement meant everything. And finally, my husband, Dale Hiestand, whose patience and never-ending belief in me keeps me going and happy.

HOW TO USE THIS BOOK

This book is written so that you, the reader, can learn how to do the skating moves both at home, where you can take your time to fully understand the body positions, and on the ice, where you will do the positions with skating speed and flow, while leaning on an edge. The illustrations of skaters and the drawings of ice tracings show in step-by-step detail how to perform these skating moves.

Each part of the book fully describes how to enjoy skating at a beginner or intermediate level. In addition, by reading the next section, you can set a goal for improving your skating skills. You can easily turn to the section of the book that you want by referring to the shaded area at the outer margin of each page.

Carry this book to the rink, just as you carry your skates. If you are having trouble with a move or exercise, reread the section that explains it and practice it again. If you are taking skating lessons, share this book with your teacher and your friends; it will be an extra way to learn. If you're not taking lessons, read and practice the moves and exercises on your own.

This book will help you understand the basics of beginner and intermediate figure skating.

INTRODUCTION

Imagine gliding across the ice on one silver blade, head up and arms outstretched. You can do that! All it takes is a pair of skates, some determination, and a dream.

People of all ages love figure skating. It's fun, it's healthy, and you get to wear special outfits. Everyone admires a graceful, confident figure skater; they admire the speed and strength it takes to skate well. To do a double axel you'll travel at about twenty miles an hour and jump about five feet high and as far as six feet across the ice. That's power! That's being a real athlete.

No matter how old you are, or how good (or not-so-good) you are at other sports, you can learn the basics and enjoy figure skating. You can learn how to analyze your "tracings"—the marks your blades leave on the ice. By studying your tracings, you'll improve your skills faster than you could have imagined.

This book will take you through the learning process step by step. You'll see why so many people love this sport. Next to football, figure skating is the most popular sport to watch on television. During the Winter Olympics, it is the number-one sport that viewers watch. But it's even more exciting to do it yourself. Skating is great exercise, too.

So let's get started!

PART ONE

For Beginners
and
Occasional Skaters

CHAPTER ONE

What Is Figure Skating?

Figure skating takes skills you probably haven't needed before: balancing on a slippery surface; leaning your weight over one side of a curved, steel blade; keeping your body in just the right position at all times. Although there are other ice-rink sports—like hockey, for example—only figure skaters draw lines and circles, called "figures," on the ice. It's because of these tracings that the sport is called figure skating.

A Short History of Skating

No one knows for sure how skating began or who was the first brave soul to put something like a blade under his or her feet and step onto the ice. It is generally believed that skating began as a form of transportation over lakes, rivers, and streams. The earliest skates were found in a lake in Switzerland. They have been examined and are believed to date back to 3000 B.C.

Back in the seventeenth century, hunters from Scandinavian countries made their own ice skates. They made the boots out of leather. The blades were hand-carved from the materials they could find most easily—bone from reindeer, elk, horses, and even walrus tusks. In 1848, the bone blades were replaced by steel and the shape of the blade changed. Until that time, skates were simply used for transportation, and the hand-carved blades had a straight, flat shape. The new steel blade had a curve, a shape that allowed the skater to make fancy figures on the ice. A new type of skating emerged—a sport, not just a way to travel. The new activity was called figure skating in English and artistic skating in many other languages.

Drawing figures on the ice proved to be a an enjoyable—and challenging!—pastime. Skillful skaters made figures by moving their bodies while balancing on their curved blades. They drew fish, swans, trees, fancy letters, and, of course, figure eights, as well as many variations of the figure eight. Their figure eights were small, with the diameter about the height of the skater.

A lot of people caught the skating fever and tried more complicated figures. One skate manufacturing company, The Barney and Berry Company of Springfield, Massachusetts, made over 600,000 pairs of clamp-on skates *every year* from 1865 to 1919!

A clever American nineteenth-century skater, Jackson Haines, wanted to do more than just draw figures on the ice.

"Winter"—A Skating Scene (courtesy New York Public Library)

Born in Chicago in 1840, he had been a balletmaster, and he decided to bring the turns, jumps, and spins of the classical ballet tradition to figure skating. Haines had toe picks added to the front of the blade so a skater could grip the ice surface, spring up into a jump, and then balance on the blade—not just for a turn, but also to spin in place like a top. Because of him, and because of the introduction of toe picks, figure skating became more than an art of making tracings on the ice; it became a competitive athletic sport with daring jumps, fast spins, and other beautiful moves.

Until 1977, figures were an important part of competitive figure skating. There were over sixty different figures, all based on the original figure eight made by two circles connected at one spot. The simplest figure eight required a skater to skate in a circle, first on one foot, then on the other, connecting the two circles at the point of origin. More complex figures involved turns, changes of edge, and other techniques. Skaters were judged on the accuracy of these required figure eights, known as compulsory figures, which accounted for up to forty percent of the overall score in a competition. Skaters had to be proficient at doing their figures in order to do well in their ratings.

Between 1977 and 1991, the officials who govern the sport of figure skating gradually eliminated figures from competition. The International Skating Union decided that figure skating competitions would be more exciting for spectators without the compulsory figures. Not everyone agreed with this decision at the time, and coaches still argue about whether the ISU made the correct decision. Many teachers believe that figures are as important to a skater as the scales of the piano are to a pianist—they teach timing, positions, and discipline—and that there would be fewer injuries in figure skating if skaters practiced figures.

Clothing for skating performances has changed drastically twice in the history of figure skating. In the 1920s, an attractive Norwegian girl named Sonja Henie wanted to appear more like a ballerina than an outdoor ballroom dancer like her predecessors. She shocked and entertained her worldwide audiences with her custom-made skating dresses that ended just above her knee—not at the ankle, as was the fashion. Audiences approved and other female skaters followed her lead, thus changing the style of dressing. Sonja Henie went on to win three Olympic medals!

Then, starting slowly in the middle 1960s, another change occurred, thanks to the interest in broadcasting skating events for television viewers. Arena lights became brighter, making the temperature too warm for heavy velvet and taffeta long-sleeved costumes. At the same time, manufacturers developed synthetic fabrics that could stretch with a skater's moves. Performers switched to chiffon and spandex fabrics. Short-sleeved and sleeveless outfits, decorated with sequins and rhinestones that reflected the light, became popular. Glamour and a sense of lightness added to the spectacle.

FIGURE SKATING TODAY

Figure skating today involves much more than drawing figures on the ice. It features jumping, rotating in the air, performing fancy footwork, and interpreting music. The sport continues to grow and change, and, in spite of the fact that figures are no longer judged as part of figure skating, the original name of the sport—"figure skating"—is still used.

Figure skating is like dancing: you can perform as a soloist, with a partner, or as part of a group. You may find another skater or a group of skaters that you like to skate with, since it's fun to do things with your friends, and you can help each other learn. Whether your goal is to be a star or just to skate with friends from time to time, it's important to learn to balance properly, use your edges, get up after a fall, and come to a safe stop. Once you learn the basics, you can choose which type of figure skating you want to do.

The sport of ice dancing might appeal to you. Ice dancing is like ballroom dancing, but it takes place on ice. Years of practice are required to dance with ease and grace, the way the Olympic stars do, but there are recreational ice dancers, too. Ice dancing sessions are often part of the regular weekly schedules of local skating clubs. Skaters do fox-trots, waltzes, tangos, cha-chas, and many other ballroom dances, each with its own steps and patterns. Many skaters enjoy the social aspects of ice dancing.

Although advanced ice dancers do jumps and spins, the rules of competitive ice dancing limit these moves so that ice dancing isn't confused with pair skating. Pair skaters do jumps and spins together at high speed over the ice. In certain lifts, the girl's head can be about ten feet from the ice. If her partner loses his grip on her, or loses his balance, she can have a nasty fall. Pair skaters train with helmets—and you can see why.

Synchronized team skating is a good choice for skaters who are good at the basics, who like doing things in a group, and who are able to put in the necessary practice time. Synchronized skating groups perform during quarter time at hockey games, in competitions as a synchronized skating team, and in the chorus lines of skating shows.

OTHER SKATING SPORTS ON ICE

Two other sports take place on ice: hockey and speed skating. As in figure skating, these sports use a boot with an attached blade, but they have very different objectives, rules, and equipment.

Hockey is great for kids who like team sports. As a hockey player, you have to be quick on your feet and able to skate with power while looking in all directions. The hockey skate is built to allow deep knee and ankle bending so the skater can travel over the ice as fast and as safely as possible. Unlike figure skates, the hockey skate doesn't have a high heel; it is flat. Some skaters are simply more comfortable in hockey skates. Both girls and boys like hockey because of the teamwork it involves.

Hockey players must learn to protect their bodies against other skaters, the rink's railing, hockey sticks, and flying hockey pucks. Players wear sturdy helmets and protect their faces with face and mouth guards. The rest of their bodies are covered with pads to protect their shoulders, elbows, hands, fingers, shins, lower spine, hip, thighs, knees, and torsos. Goalies wear all that plus goalie skates, which have a protective shell, and special gloves for both catching the puck and using the stick to fend it off. Hockey pucks can travel over one hundred miles per hour.

The blade of a hockey skate has a curve, but it doesn't have toe picks like the figure skate blade; it's not made for doing jumps and spins. Whereas the toe picks of the figure skate blade dig into the ice on the takeoff and landing, the curve of the hockey blade is just right for quick changes of direction, sharp corners, and crossovers.

Speed skating is another ice sport. Speed skates are designed for racing, so there are not many moves you can do with them other than forward skating and forward crossovers. You can't really *stop* with speed skates; you just slow down. Competitive speed skaters move even faster than figure skaters or hockey players. A speed skater's stretch outfit, from the hood to the toe coverings, is aerodynamically designed to allow the skater to move through the air with the least possible resistance.

The boot of a speed skate is cut low, with no heel lift, and the blade is fifteen inches long, more than one-and-a-half times the length of a figure or hockey blade. The two edges are very close together. Unlike figure or hockey blades, which are sharpened so that both edges are even, each blade of a speed skate is sharpened at an angle to give the most speed when the skater is racing counterclockwise. The left outside edge and the right inside edge are lower to the ice than the left inside edge and the right outside edge. A speed-skate blade is like the blade of a knife—long and sharp. For this reason, speed skaters wear protective gear around their necks to protect themselves in the event of a collision with another skater.

Practicing speed skating at a competitive level is difficult because only a few rinks are large enough. Most speed skating rinks are located at sport centers that have hosted the Olympic Winter Games. Official figure skating competitions and hockey games use standard rinks, which are smaller—about one hundred feet wide by two hundred feet long.

By learning the basic skills of figure skating, you will also be learning the basics of hockey, and speed skating. No learning time will be lost; once you've mastered the basics, you can choose which kind of skating you want to do. And whenever you get the chance, you'll lace up those skates and glide across the ice . . . head up and smiling!

WHERE TO SKATE: RINKS OR PONDS

Pictures of smiling skaters enjoying themselves on ponds or lakes make great holiday cards, but natural bodies of water have two big disadvantages compared with artificially frozen ice rinks: the ice of a pond is not smooth—and it may not be safe. Never skate alone on a pond, and never skate on one without safety equipment, including a ladder. Don't skate on ponds that are not properly maintained. Make sure the ice is solidly frozen before you even think of skating on it. If you see children skating on a pond, find an adult and ask if it's safe to skate there. It's always better to play it safe. If you're not sure, don't skate there!

Artificially frozen ice rinks, whether indoor or outdoor, are always safe, and the consistency of their ice makes your practice sessions easier and more comfortable. Rinks use a special vehicle to keep the surface smooth. Skaters refer to this ice resurfacing vehicle as a "Zamboni" because the Zamboni Company made the first ones. The word is also used as a verb; skaters say, "They are zamboni-ing the ice."

Most ice rinks are what we call Olympic-size—one hundred feet wide by two hundred feet long. Under this large area of frozen ice are miles and miles of refrigeration pipes, similar to the ones in a home refrigerator. These pipes keep the ice at a controlled, even temperature and a consistent texture for skating. Many sport centers today build two rinks, one for ice hockey and one for figure skating. Hockey players prefer very hard ice, while figure skaters like "softer" ice, with some spring to it.

Ice rinks have one more advantage over ponds and lakes: most of them have a bulletin board. Skaters use bulletin boards to exchange information and help each other. You'll see lots of notices for buying and selling skates and other equipment, skating clubs you can join, competitions, recitals, and lessons. While you're checking out the bulletin board, you will meet and talk with other skaters, their friends, and parents. You can learn a lot of useful things there.

YOUR BODY: YOUR ESSENTIAL SKATING TOOL

The piece of equipment you'll rely on most to learn figure skating isn't your skates, it's your body. Before thinking about skates—which to buy, where to buy, whether to rent or buy—you should know what to expect from yourself when you skate.

The body is what makes figure skating happen. Figure skating is based on your body leaning over on one of the two edges of your steel blade. You have probably seen bicycles or motorcycles leaning over as their riders go around a curve. Your body will do the same thing when you skate. Understanding and feeling how your body is leaning—and how skating is based on this lean to make curved tracings—is the most important part of understanding figure skating.

When a skater is on an edge, his or her body is in a straight line, from the middle of the head to one of the two edges of the blade. And that straight line is tilted either to the right or to the left. Skating moves are made by the position of the body over the blade. The line cut on the ice is the result of the position of the body. Just as your hand controls a pencil when you write, your body controls the blade when you lean. Both the pencil and the blade leave a mark. In skating, this mark is called a tracing.

In order to hold the correct body positions in skating, and to skate safely, you need to understand five posture points. They are your head, your back, your arms, the leg you are skating on, and the leg that is off the ice. Finding these positions by standing in your socks in front of a mirror is the most effective way to get what trainers call "muscle memory." To skate well, you first need to know what the position you're in feels like to you, and then memorize that position so you can do it on the ice as well. The basic positions will soon become second nature to you.

Posture Point #1: Your Head

Hold your head so that your chin is parallel to the floor (pretend the floor is the ice). In this position, you can lower your eyes to see the ice close to you, and you can also see ahead. Your head is the heaviest part of your body; it weighs about seven pounds. If it isn't in the right position, it will throw off your balance enough to slow your progress tremendously, or even make you fall.

Beginners or skaters learning a new move will often, out of tension, let the head drop forward so they can look down. If you do this, you have about seven pounds of weight in the wrong spot when you are trying to do a move. Remind yourself frequently not to look down. When your head is up with your chin level with the ice, you look like a confident skater. You are doing something else too: you are releasing the tension between your shoulder blades. The less tension you have in your body, the easier it is to move.

Right from the beginning, get in the habit of looking to the end of your rink as you skate. This is a safe position, in that you can see ahead and anticipate any changes in direction that you might need to make. Looking ahead like this is what you do when you ride a bicycle. You don't look right over your handlebars; you look ahead to avoid obstacles and to anticipate a change. It is the same with figure skating: keep your eyes looking ahead.

Posture Point #2: Your Back

Like the stem of a flower, the back holds up the body. People are born with differently shaped backs. The shape of the back is one of the things that separates the style of one skater from another. Some people have what we call bad posture, but it can be improved by learning new habits and breaking old ones. Skating will improve your posture.

When you skate, your back should feel like a straight line from the top of the neck down to the tailbone. People sometimes incorrectly sway their backs by pushing their chests out, allowing their upper backs to "sit" into the lower back. In this position you are not in correct balance. It prevents mastering the smooth and fluid movement you will be aiming to do.

To understand balance, look at your body in front of a mirror. Stand sideways so that one shoulder is closer to the mirror. Have your feet lined up and touching one another. Inhale, and then, as you exhale, pull in your lower abdominal muscles and sink into your ankles, as if your back is sliding down a wall. When you look in the mirror, you will see that your knees are directly over your toes. Your arms will be out to the sides for balance. Now, in this position, make sure your chin is parallel to

the floor. Bring your head back, just the smallest amount. Take deep breaths in this position. Then, with your eyes closed, continue to take deep breaths. Work on memorizing how this position feels. Come up in your knees after a minute or two, and then repeat. Make sure your abdominal muscles are held tightly. Proper bending starts with tight abdominal muscles.

Body alignment without skates on

Posture Point #3: Your Arms

There are two reasons to have your arms out to your sides. Both reasons are for safety: your arms help you to balance, and they establish your space on the ice so that other skaters don't come too close.

To feel the correct position of the arms for forward skating, stand facing a mirror. Imagine a clock around your body with twelve o'clock in front and six o'clock behind you. Stretch your arms out to your sides, towards three o'clock on your right side, and towards nine o'clock on your left. Your fingertips should be at about hip level. Bend your elbows ever so slightly so that the arms have a soft curve to them. Now your arms are in the right position.

Your wrists should be relaxed and not bent. The palms of your hands should be facing toward the ground. Keep your wrists soft and relaxed as well. If your wrists are bent upward, the palms of your hands will be parallel to the ice. This is dangerous! If you were to fall in that position, you would hit the ice with that tense angle at your wrist, causing too much impact to the wrist area. If you fall while your palms are in a continuous

Is Your Arm Position Correct?

- Make sure you are standing tall.
- Your head should be held straight, with your chin line parallel to the floor and your eyes looking directly ahead.
- Extend your arms at hip level toward three o'clock and nine o'clock. Arms should look and feel relaxed.
- Now, wiggle your fingers. You should be able to see them wiggling without turning your head.

line with your arms, your hands are able to slide and help cushion the impact.

Posture Point #4: The Leg You Are Skating on

Skating teachers don't refer to the sides of your body as left and right, but as your skating side and free side. If you are balancing on your left foot, the left foot is the skating foot; the left leg is the skating leg; the left hip the skating hip, and so on. The right foot, in this position, is called the free foot; the right leg the free leg, etc. The opposite terms would be used if you were skating on your right foot.

Pressing into your skating ankle causes you to bend the skating knee. As you bend your ankle, keep your knee directly over it; don't let the knee lean inward or outward. If you're not careful, it is easy for the knee to fall in toward the center of the body. Many people blame this awkward position on "weak ankles," but that's not really the problem. It's not weak ankles, but improper bending of the ankle that make your ankles turn inward. This is, unfortunately, a very common mistake, but you can catch it by standing in front of a mirror, bending your ankle, and checking that your knee is right over your toes. Don't be

How to Bend

- Stand on both feet with your ankles and knees slightly bent.
- Think about your lower abdominal muscles as you pull them in tightly.
- Pull your upper body up to feel the length of your back.
- As you pull up, feel the separation of your shoulder blades as they reach toward the outside of your body.
- Feel your tailbone tuck down and under.
- Keep your arms relaxed and out to your sides.

Now you're getting closer to the real bending part. Start breathing more deeply—in through your nose and out your mouth.

- While exhaling, push your knees down as you bend your ankles even more.
- Press your thigh muscles down.
- Let your toes spread apart and relax the feet.
- Feel your shoulders over your hips.
- Imagine that the hair on top of your head is pulled upward at the same time that your lower body is pressing downward.
- Continue breathing deeply.
- Make sure your abdominal muscles are still tight.

Now, memorize this feeling! This is what we mean when we say the simple word *bend.*

afraid of bending too much; most skaters take years to bend sufficiently. While you are in front of the mirror and holding on to something for balance, look down to see if your knee blocks your view of the toe of the same foot. It's essential for both the knees and the ankles to bend properly.

Skating teachers and coaches probably use the word "bend" more than any other word. It's the most important word in skating; you'll hear it as long as you skate. It's not just for beginners. You'll hear coaches discussing the amount of knee bend endlessly in analyzing the jumps, spins, and flow of a top competitor's program. That one word—bend—really means "bend much more." The exercises you do in front of the mirror will help you understand the meaning of that important word.

When you do proper bending with skates on, you'll feel the front of your skate boot press firmly against your lower shin. The boot will feel tight and secure, as if it is grabbing your ankle. The boot was designed to give you this feeling, but to get it you have to bend deeply enough. In the beginning you will be constantly reminding yourself to bend. Don't worry; it will become a good habit. Your improvement rate has a lot to do with understanding and feeling the proper bend.

Posture Point #5: The Leg off the Ice

The leg you are holding off the ice (or floor, if you are practicing in front of a mirror) is called the free leg. At first your goal will simply be to keep one foot up and keep it off the ice. If you find that you are using it for balance, then correct your overall position. If you have to tap your foot on the ice to find your balance, you are not learning to correct your mistake in posture. Your aim is to extend this free leg and free foot. Begin by trying this exercise: Imagine a clock around your body. Picture where the three o'clock and four o'clock marks are. With your skating ankle and knee well bent, stretch your free foot out to four o'clock. Depending on your speed, this will generally be the position of your free leg and foot when you do basic forward skating. You should feel all the muscles on the inside of your free leg, from the inside of your thigh to your big toe. When you really use the muscles of your free leg, you feel as if you are pointing with your free toe, just as you would point a finger.

The angle at which your leg is stretched out from your body depends on the speed you are going at the time. Here's an angle that works well with slow skating:

- Stand in front of your mirror with your chin level so that your eyes are looking straight ahead, your back is tall and straight, your arms are out, your fingertips are at hip level, and both ankles are bent.

- Imagine a clock around your body. Twelve o'clock will be in front of you.

- Bring your right leg out to three o'clock.

- Lift your right leg ever so slightly off the floor with your free leg muscles fully stretched (you might need to hold onto a chair at this point).

- As you look ahead into the mirror, slowly and carefully bring your free leg from three o'clock to almost four o'clock (the exact angle varies with skaters and with speed).

- Concentrate on moving the free foot, *without allowing the hips to turn to your right*.

Controlling the hips like this is called having "square hips." If your hips are not square, you will be fighting for balance. This is the position that the Olympic skaters work so hard on when they are skating about twenty miles an hour and preparing for a double, triple, or quad jump. At the exact point of takeoff for a jump, they need square hips. You are working on feeling square hips right now. This feeling will always be a part of your skating.

Muscle Memory

Now that you have mastered these five posture points in front of your mirror, you are ready for the next step: to memorize

> ### Tip: Kitchen Skating
>
> Practice the five posture points at home on the kitchen floor while wearing socks. On a slippery floor you can twist and glide a little, while using the counter for support, to get the feel of being on the ice.

these positions. Your goal is to create what is called muscle memory. Every skating coach insists on creating muscle memory.

To do so, take your time. Go over the posture points with your eyes closed. Breathe deeply. Think of your body as a whole with every part in the correct position. When you rent or buy your first skates, stand in them, bend properly, and focus on your posture points. You will be able to get a good fit because you know what to expect from your body. Your body is more important than your skates as a tool for learning. Make it work right! Good posture is the essential tool that you need before getting the next important tool: your skates.

SKATES: TO RENT OR TO BUY

The fit of your skates is very important. You can get a good fit in rental skates as well as in skates that you buy. When deciding whether to rent or buy, consider how often you plan to skate and how comfortable you feel in rented skates. Some skaters discover that they like their rented skates so much, they want to buy them. Rented skates are better than you would expect. Rink owners want skaters to keep coming back, so they are careful about the quality and maintenance of their rental skates. You may be surprised how well trained the skate rental staff are at choosing your correct skate size. They know that an incorrect fit or unsharpened blades can make for an unhappy skater who won't return.

Poorly fitted skates can make you believe that you have weak ankles. Weak ankles are very uncommon. Skaters who think they have weak ankles usually have poorly fitted skates or poorly supported ankles, or they are not bending properly. If your skates don't hug your ankles, your ankles will fall toward the inside of your feet. If this happens, get a tighter fit by choosing a smaller size skate, or use a skate that has better support. For beginners, I recommend that you rent skates until you are experienced enough to know what you need. Learn the basics on rentals and then you will be ready to buy your own skates.

YOUR FIRST PAIR OF SKATES

Beginners who are new to skating can choose from two types of figure skates: the recreational skate and the traditional skate. Each has its pros and cons. You'll have to decide whether comfort (which is easier to find in a recreational skate) or progress (which will come more readily with traditional skates) is more important to you. With either type of skate, your main concern is that it should fit snugly over your ankle area. The blades of both the recreational and the traditional skate have toe picks that allow you to jump and to balance when spinning.

The recreational skate

The Recreational Skate

The recreational skate (also called a leisure or soft skate) comes with the blade attached to the boot. It is generally less expensive, and often more comfortable for the skater who doesn't skate regularly. The boot part of the skate has more canvas than leather. Since leather is stiffer, you are getting less support from a recreational skate than you would get from a traditional skate. The best feature of the recreational skate is the easy adjustment from your normal footwear. If you wear sneakers often and are comfortable in them, you'll be right at home in the recreational skate, because it is constructed very much like a sneaker.

If you're going to limit your skating to occasional sessions or skating once or twice a season, the recreational skate will fit your needs. It is easy to wear and yet has enough support for forward crossovers and for stopping safely. However, if you expect to be doing more than basic forward skating and crossovers, I recommend that you get the traditional figure skate.

The Traditional Skate

This is the skate to get if you skate often and want to make a lot of progress. In the traditional figure-skating boot, you can buy the leather boot and blade together, as in the recreational skate; or you can buy the boot and blade separately. For your first pair of skates, a figure skate with the blade attached to the boot is a

Recreational vs. Traditional Skates

Recreational skate	Traditional skate
Boot and blade come together	Boot and blade sold together or separately
Boot made of canvas and leather	All-leather boot
Easy to adjust to	Better support
For occasional skating	For more frequent skating
Good for very basic skating	Better for progressing to higher skill levels

good choice. When you are more advanced and are "doing edges" with speed and confidence, you will probably want to buy the boot and blade separately.

The traditional skate

BUYING SKATES

This is a big step, and you want to make the right choice so you will be happy with your skates for a long time. There are lots of pointers, but no matter how much you know, you have to judge the feel of the skate for yourself. Whether you have chosen the recreational skate or the traditional skate, you will be looking for the same thing: a good fit.

Start off by wearing the right socks when you try on skates. Thin, cotton socks or tights are best. You might think that heavy wool socks would keep your feet from getting cold, but they interfere with the way your skates fit. Thick socks work well with hockey skates and with ski boots, but not with figure skates, because figure skates have to fit tightly over the ankle. Wearing thick socks allows the foot to move around inside the boot, which can make it more difficult to find your balance. That is why skaters who skate outdoors in cold weather keep their feet warm by wearing covers, made of insulated fabric or fur (real or fake), over their boots.

The best place to buy skates is a shop at the rink where you plan to skate. There you can not only try on the skates, but even skate in them to see how they feel. If your rink doesn't have a skate shop, a sport shop is second best. Here you can expect to find an experienced salesperson and a good selection of skates. But remember, even the best salesperson can't be as good as

Allow Your Ankles to Bend

Skates for a beginner must allow the skater's ankles to bend. If the skates are too stiff, ask for a boot with less support.

you when it comes to judging what the skate feels like on your foot.

Discount stores are the least desirable places to buy skates. The skates they sell are often defective in some way. The blades may be too short, or the hooks for the laces may be loose or already torn off. If you do shop in a discount store, examine the skates carefully before you purchase them.

Although figure skates range in price just as shoes do, the more expensive skates aren't more fashionable or prettier, they give you more support. As a beginner, you don't need a lot of support. Strong support is necessary when you are doing double and triple revolution jumps. A beginner should be looking for less support. That's good news, because it puts a beginner's choices into the lower price range.

The size you try on will probably be one to one-and-a-half sizes smaller than your shoe size. Skate and shoe sizes do not correspond, which can cause a lot of confusion. As you get ready to try on the skate, make sure the laces are loose. You want to be able to slide your foot into the skate without a struggle. When your foot is all the way inside the boot, pull the tongue toward you. Make sure your heel is down in the heel area of the boot. Before you tighten the laces, stretch out your toes and then bend them slightly. If you don't have enough room to do this, the boot is too small. If you can bend your toes all the way under, the boot is too large.

LACING YOUR SKATES

The purpose of those long laces—each one is about two yards in length—is to adjust the tightness in two different ways: to make the boot tight *at* the ankle, and looser *above* the ankle. You need the ankle area to be tight so that you are well supported, and you need the top part to be loose enough that it doesn't restrict your bending. The lowest part of the lacing (nearest your toes) seldom needs to be adjusted unless you are skating at full speed and doing advanced moves.

Skaters of all ages should lace their own skates. There are two reasons for this. First, only the skater is at the correct angle to pull on the laces most effectively; and second, only the skater can feel how tight or loose the laces are. Experienced skaters vary in the way they lace their skates. There is no one rule for everyone. How it feels to you is what matters. By stretching out your leg, you will be able to pull on the laces easily. With your hands holding the laces tightly, pull toward yourself. At this angle it is easier for you to do than for someone trying to help you.

Lacing the middle part of the boot

Lacing Up

- Stretch out the leg of the foot that you will be lacing first. As you look at your boot, visually divide it into three parts—the bottom, the middle, and the top.

- In the bottom third the laces should feel firm but not tight. They shouldn't have any loops in them, because the heel of the other blade could catch in overly loose laces, causing a scare or a fall. If they are too tight, you will see that the tongue is pinched.

- The middle part of the lacing is the most important. It will cover two or three of the eyelets and half of the hooks of the boot. This section is crucial for supporting your body. If the ankle is well supported, the body will be supported in a straight line over it. Without this support, a true lean of one line from the top of your head to the skating edge will be frustratingly difficult.

Using a Skate Hook

Some skaters use a skate hook, a tool shaped like the letter J, on the middle part of the lacing. They feel that a skate hook helps them pull tighter than they can with their fingers alone. Other skaters think they can tighten their laces better by trusting what they feel in their hands. Try both ways and decide which works best for you.

As you are lacing up the middle part of the boot, keep an eye on the tongue. It should be right in the middle of the opening between the two sides of the boot. If you see that it is slipping to one side, go back a few eyelets or hooks and place the tongue in the middle. As you lace up, try to keep the tongue flat, not wrinkled, and keep it in place. The more you do this the easier it becomes, and eventually the tongue becomes reshaped to fit your foot. Lace up this middle part tightly, using your strength. Hold your hands or skate hook close to your boot as you pull the laces toward you. When you get to the part between the eyelets and the hooks, don't let up on your force-

What to Wear for Skating

- Dress in layers so that as you warm up, you can remove a layer at a time.
- Wear wool, cotton, or silk.
- Avoid synthetic fabrics. They will not keep you warm.
- Don't wear loose clothing that might trip you.
- Girls may want to wear a long sweater on top and a leotard, along with tights.
- If you wear slacks, make sure they are made of stretch fabric, so you can bend easily in them.
- Wear thin socks or tights.

SAFETY, COMFORT, CLOTHING AND ACCESSORIES

You should always wear a helmet when you're learning how to skate. Even if you are skating at a slow beginner's speed, catching your toe pick can cause you to lose your balance. A fall can be painful. Ice is hard, but a helmet will make a fall less serious if you hit your head.

Wrist guards are another good form of protection. Harmless falls are actually slides that are most often cushioned by your hands, so it's important to protect them. Gloves are important because touching cold ice with your bare hands is very uncomfortable. Knee and elbow pads are also smart choices. Advanced figure skaters wear padded tights to protect their hips in case a poor landing ends in a fall.

When you skate, dress in layers, as you would for a cold-weather walk. Your clothing should be loose enough so you are not restricted, yet tight enough so that no extra folds in your clothing can hamper your movement. Skaters can trip on their own clothing when they wear baggy sweat pants or jeans—often the loose cuffs will become damp or wet and will stretch enough to drag on the ice. When the skaters do a quick turn, the blade can go over this part of their clothing and down they go.

To protect your blades, you'll need two types of covers. After each practice session, wipe your blades with a small absorbent towel or chamois cloth, then put terry-cloth covers on your blades to absorb any leftover moisture. These covers are called soakies. They are available at most skate shops.

You'll also need blade guards made of plastic or rubber. These fit over your blades but touch them only at the ends. They protect your blades when you are carrying your skates. If the blades rub on each other, the friction can cause a nick in the steel. The tiniest nick, right where you are balancing on the blade, can cause you to lose your lean.

If your rink has clean rubber mats, you will not need to wear blade guards while walking to and from the ice. Later, when you are more advanced and spending more money on expensive blades—perhaps even sending your blades to another state to be sharpened—you will not take any chances of dulling your blades. Skaters have been heard to say that they wish they could walk on their hands from the dressing room to the ice to save their blades from the slightest nick! This is an exaggeration, but serious skaters have good reasons to want to protect their blades.

CARING FOR YOUR BOOTS, BLADES, AND EQUIPMENT

The longer you have your skates, the more you will love them. The boots will mold to your feet, and will become more and more comfortable. You want to do everything you can to make them last until you outgrow them.

To clean the boot part of a traditional skate, just use a mild soap and a little water, followed by white or black shoe polish (whichever matches your boots). If you have recreational skates, you will clean the boot part with plain soap and water. Some skaters use an old toothbrush to scrub the difficult parts of their boots.

Wipe your blades after every skating session. Put your soakies on the wiped blades to absorb any remaining moisture.

When you feel you are "slipping off your edge"—and you're sure it's not because of a lack of speed or a less than perfect position—you might be ready for a skate sharpening. Run your finger lightly over your blades. If you feel any nicks, particularly on the middle section of your blade, your skates are due for a sharpening. Don't press too hard as you run your fingers over your blades. If your blades are sharper than you thought, you can cut your finger and draw blood; it feels like a paper cut. If that happens, you'll know that the blade is pretty sharp. Dull or badly nicked blades should be brought to a professional blade sharpener.

When your skates are sharpened, the hollow in between the two edges is redefined. Sharpenings are measured in sixteenths of an inch. As a beginner, you are safe to ask for a half-inch sharpening. That means the tool that redefines the hollow between the two edges has a radius of half an inch. A deeper sharpening, for an intermediate skater who skates regularly once a week, would be seven-sixteenths. Serious skaters, who skate almost every day, would choose a three-eighths-of-an-inch sharpening. Keep a log of your blade sharpenings to record what measurement was used, how many hours of skating it took you to adjust to the sharper blades, and how long the sharpening lasted. For a beginner who skates less than once a week, a half-inch sharpening should last nine to twelve months.

TIPS FOR SMOOTH SKATING

A good blade sharpener will check the screws that attach your blade to your boot, as these can become loose. A loose blade is dangerous to skate on. If you lose a screw while skating, your blade can wobble, causing you to lose your balance—and if another skater skates over the screw, he or she can fall as well. Get in the habit of checking the tightness of your screws. Keep an appropriate screwdriver in your skate bag or locker in case you need it.

Wash your soakies with soap and water. If you don't, you are putting your blades into protection material that is not clean. Your soakies can be washed by hand or in a washing machine.

> ### *Take Care of Yourself*
>
> The most important piece of equipment to take care of is your body. Keep it in tip-top shape with healthy eating habits. Avoid rink food; it's usually not nutritious. Stay away from junk food in general. Get enough rest, and get exercise that's fun to do. How about figure skating?

Grit can form in your blade guards. As you walk, the toe picks and heel of your blade will press into this grit and become dull. Blades also become dull by skating on rough ice or by walking without blade guards on unclean rubber mats. (Of course, walking on anything harder than rubber—like wood, plastic or metal—will quickly dull and nick your blades.) Scrub your blade guards with a toothbrush using soap and water.

CHAPTER TWO

ALMOST READY TO MOVE

You're getting ready to skate! You'll be moving in a very short time.

In this chapter you'll be introduced to some more basic ideas that are important in skating. You'll learn more about edges and tracings, how to read and write the shorthand that skaters use when learning and studying their moves, rink dos and don'ts, and skating etiquette. We'll finish with some tips on how to overcome the many fears that can bother you when you skate, and then a brief warm-up exercise that you can make a part of your skating habits.

EDGES AND FLATS

Figure skating is the art of making beautiful curves on the ice—curves that happen because the body leans. This lean of the body is one straight line from the middle of the skater's head to the outside or inside edge of his or her blade. Leaning is done while skating both forward and backward, and on both the right and the left foot. Learning to lean is the way you learn to skate on your edges. And edges are what makes skating so exciting.

As your body changes from one lean to another—for example, from an outside lean to an inside lean—the edge also changes. During this short period of transition, your body will be straight over your blade and you will be on both edges. This is called "being on a flat." If you look at the tracing of a flat, it will be two lines, an equal distance apart—the same exact distance between the two edges of your blade, about an eighth of an inch.

If you are skating on a flat, you are probably going straight ahead or straight backward. Skating on a flat is fine—in fact, it's great—when you are a beginner. More advanced moves are done on curves instead of straight lines. As you progress you will be working to use more edges, and fewer unnecessary flats, in your skating.

You can't get on an edge if you are standing still or moving too slowly. Edges depend on a certain amount of speed. But as you progress with your skating and learn to go faster, you'll begin to lean without realizing it at first.

When you are on an edge—for instance, on your left forward outside edge—and your body is in the proper position, you will feel the line of your lean. You will learn to love this feeling.

The proper body position for leaning:

- **Head and eyes straight ahead**
- **Back straight**
- **Arms out so that the finger tips are at hip level**
- **Skating knee and ankle bent**
- **Free foot extended**

Memorize this body position. If your skating is not smooth, make sure you have enough speed and refocus on these five points of body position.

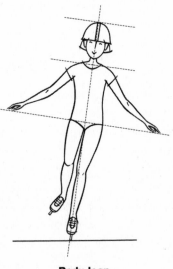

Body lean

USING TRACINGS TO ANALYZE YOUR EDGES

You have chosen a sport that is unique. Only figure skaters can study a written record of every move they make by looking at the marks they leave. Your tracings will tell you exactly what you did right and what went wrong. No other sport makes it so easy for the student and the coach to work together.

When compulsory figure eights were a part of competition, judges would get down on their hands and knees, studying the ice to see if an edge was clean. Skaters lost points if they were skating on one edge, but the edge on the other side of the blade—just one eighth of an inch away—touched the ice! Just as the judges used tracings to study the precision of a move, you can use your tracings to improve your skating skills. The ice always tells the truth clearly and objectively.

An expression used often by instructors, professionals, and television commentators is the "quality of a skater's edges." When they say this, they are talking about how well the edges glide over the ice. "No scraping" is a good sign. Scraping is the sound of a skate sliding sideways on the ice; it will leave a little pile of snow on one side of the tracing as a sign that something wasn't quite right. In free-style skating competitions, both in singles and in pairs, judges today still look closely to see if there is a scrape before a turn, lift, or a jump.

As a skater, you will develop several very acute senses. The first will be the sense of balance. Second is the sense of feeling a lean. Next comes your sense of hearing. You will learn to listen to the sound of your blade moving on the ice and you will become able to analyze that sound. Good-quality edges are quiet. Silent skating means that the skater's body is aligned over the blade's edge and the skater is moving at a good speed. When you find yourself using these senses, you can pat yourself on the back and say, "I'm a skater now."

In ice dancing, tracings have extra importance. The steps of each dance follow a pattern of tracings on the ice. There are about twenty different ice dance patterns, and each one has its own set of required tracings.

Throughout your skating you will look for your tracings. By studying them, you will learn to recognize the shapes that are made by the various skating moves. Look for consistency in shape, size and curvature. With practice, you will train your eye to learn the lessons of tracings at a glance. When you can do that, you will learn to love your tracings and be grateful for them. Without tracings you would not be able to see your mistakes. Get in the habit of reading your tracings to analyze and improve your skating moves.

THE ABCs OF SKATING ABBREVIATIONS

When solo and pair skaters choreograph their programs, they draw the tracings of the moves they plan to do on paper. They represent each move with a three-letter abbreviation. You'll want to learn these abbreviations for several reasons:

- They help you understand skating moves described in books.
- They help you write down the moves you are learning.
- They help you communicate quickly and easily with your coach and with other skaters.

Basic skating language is universal. All pros and coaches use the terms "skating side" and "free side" instead of "right side" and "left side." They try not to use the word "right," because it can mean the opposite of "left" or the opposite of "wrong," which could be confusing. Similarly, all pros and coaches use the same abbreviations to quickly tell their students which foot, direction, and edge they should be using.

If you are on your right foot, going forward, on the outside edge, this is called RFO—R is for your right foot, F for the forward direction, and O for your outside edge.

F can also be for flat, meaning being on both edges at once. When it means "flat," instead of "forward," it is always the third letter of the abbreviation.

Here are the abbreviations and what they mean:

For forward skating:

RFO — Right forward outside
LFO — Left forward outside
RFI — Right forward inside
LFI — Left forward inside
RFF — Right forward flat
LFF — Left forward flat

And for back skating:

RBO — Right back outside
LBO — Left back outside
RBI — Right back inside
LBI — Left back inside
RBF — Right back flat
LBF — Left back flat

The three letters are always in the same order: first the foot you are on, then the direction, and then the edge or flat.

Understanding Skating Abbreviations

First letter	Right or left foot
Second letter	Forward or backward
Third letter	Outside edge, inside edge, or flat

When you put together your own program with your teacher, you will need to know these abbreviations so that you can translate each group of three letters into movement.

OVERCOMING FEARS AND BUILDING CONFIDENCE

Fear is one of the biggest obstacles to learning to skate. Coaches know that it is something every beginning skater has to face, and they have developed techniques for dealing with it. All skaters, at every level, have some degree of fear. From the first-time skater tentatively pushing onto one foot, to the experienced skater traveling across the ice at twenty miles an hour about to attempt a quad jump, all have a degree of fear. The big difference is that the experienced skater knows how to handle fear better than the novice skater does.

How do you cope with fear? Without doubt, having a sense of humor is one way. Learning not to dwell on your bad points also helps. After a practice session or a lesson, many skaters tend to think only about all the wrong things they did. Thinking of your good points will build your confidence, and with confidence, you will have better posture. Better posture, in itself, will improve your alignment and your skating.

Having fear is not wrong. Having *no* fear is wrong—and dangerous! When you first begin skating, fear is natural. You are nervous because you don't know what to expect. Then, as you progress, you are afraid of doing a move or a difficult jump incorrectly and risking a fall.

Here are some of the things that cause fears—and how to overcome them.

- *Not understanding.*

   This is the most common reason for fear. Make sure you fully understand what you are attempting. If you don't understand the technique, you have good reason to be fearful. If you are learning by reading this book, re-read the instructions. If you are taking lessons, ask questions. Practice the body positions of the move off the ice until you are sure you understand them.

- *Your body is stiff with tension.*

  If you are late for a skating session, you'll find yourself rushing to the rink, rushing to put on your skates, rushing out onto the ice. All this rushing makes your body tense before you even begin to skate. Always allow yourself enough time to get to the rink, change clothes, and put your skates on without rushing. Take time to do some warm-up exercises. Before you step on the ice, breathe deeply.

- *You're trying too hard.*

  Always remember why you started skating. Probably the answer is "to have fun." If you're not having fun, you are being too hard on yourself! Remind yourself to relax. Think of the positive things you've accomplished in your skating. Skaters tend to dwell on what went wrong in order to correct their mistakes. That's a good way to figure out what went wrong, but you should spend an equal amount of time patting yourself on the back for the things in skating that you do correctly.

- *You're too critical of yourself.*

  Nobody likes a person who brags out loud, but there is nothing wrong with bragging silently to yourself. Giving yourself a pep talk will help to build up your confidence; when you feel confident, you can relax and do your best.

- *You need visualization.*

  Learn what professional athletes have learned: visualization. Picture yourself doing a move that you are afraid of doing. Imagine how you look doing it today, and how you want to look when you have mastered it.

- *You don't have a goal.*

  It helps to set goals for yourself. Start with a goal for the session that you are skating. Then think about your long-term goals. At the beginning of a season, many coaches ask their students to write out their goals for the next three months, as well as the next six months. Knowing where you want to go is like having a road map. It helps both the student and the coach know where they're going. Be proud when you see your progress. Be realistic about your goals, and reward yourself when you reach them.

- *You're scared of getting hurt.*

  Don't put undue pressure on yourself. Pressure only makes your body stiff and prevents it from moving gracefully. The more pressure you put on yourself, the more your body becomes awkward and refuses to perform. It can become a vicious circle. Give yourself a break!

  The breathing exercises of yoga can help you conquer your fear. Students of yoga inhale before making an effort; they exhale when they are using their muscles and testing their physical achievement. If you apply this principle to your skating, it will help relax your body and reduce painful falls. Before your pushoff, inhale deeply. Then, as you bend your ankles and transfer your weight to the skating foot, exhale with the pushoff. Using yoga breathing when you push off from a standing position will make a big difference.

RINK RULES AND SKATING ETIQUETTE

One important way to build your skating confidence is to understand rink rules and practice good skating etiquette. When you know what's expected of you, you can relax and concentrate on

Typical skating rink rules

- Everyone must skate in a counterclockwise direction.
- No pushing, shoving, or horseplay.
- No skating more than two abreast.
- No playing crack-the-whip.
- No food or drink on the ice
- Follow the instructions of the skate guards.
- Clear the ice promptly when the session is over.
- The center of the ice is reserved for figure skaters and students taking lessons.

your moves. Using courtesy on the ice enables everyone to enjoy a better skating session.

Every rink has rules. Usually you will see them posted on a sign as you enter the ice. They are also often printed on the back of your admission ticket. The purpose of the rules is to make skating safe for you and your friends. If you don't understand the rules, ask a rink guard or the manager.

For you as a figure skater, the most important rule is the one that concerns the use of center of the rink. You will often see this area set apart by brightly colored plastic cones. This is the area where you will take your lessons and practice your moves. At other times, of course, you'll want to practice your forward and backward skating in the outer area of the rink, which is known as "the track."

When you skate in the track, be aware that many beginners will be holding onto the railing for support. Skate well away from the railing so they won't be in your way. At first, as a beginner, you will skate slowly, and other skaters will pass you.

A skating party at the rink

Looking for a great place to have a birthday party or other celebration? Ask the manager of your ice rink about having a party there. Many rinks have a party room and the staff can help you with balloons, cakes, and treats.

After you've learned to skate with some speed, you will in turn pass slower skaters. Be sure to allow plenty of space in case they make a sudden move or fall. Keeping your head up, look ahead to anticipate any potential dangers.

Rink guards cut quickly through the center when they need to help a skater who has fallen down and is a danger to others. If you are practicing in the center, keep an eye out for the guards. In most rinks their colorful jackets make them easy to spot.

Never skate recklessly. If you are practicing and you feel that a skater is being reckless, tell the skate guard or the manager of the rink.

When you skate at a new rink, always check the rules of the rink. They are for your safety as well as that of others. And what if there are advanced skaters whizzing past you and doing fancy moves? The best way to get along with other skaters is to compliment them on their moves. You can also ask them how they learned certain things or comment on the progress they've made. You'll make friends quickly this way—and have more fun on the ice.

The Zamboni

If you've watched a figure skating show, competition, or a hockey game, you've probably seen the "Zamboni," the fascinating machine on thick rubber wheels that cleans the ice. This mechanical marvel scrapes the ice down to make it level and then picks up the ice scrapings as it spreads down a film of hot water. As the water freezes, it leaves a layer of perfectly smooth new ice behind. The Zamboni goes about eight miles an hour. Resurfacing a full-size rink takes about fifteen to thirty minutes.

Frank Zamboni, the father of an ice dancer named Joan Zamboni, invented the ice-resurfacing machine in 1947. He was a rink operator and rink owner but never skated himself.

Before the Zamboni, it took a lot more time and work to resurface the ice, and the result wasn't as good. In some rinks, it took six men with enormous shovels and squeegees up to an hour and a half to make new ice. First, men pushing shovels cleared away the used or "dirty" ice. Then, one man would spray the ice surface with hot water from a large hose, similar to a fireman's hose. Finally, six men would spread the hot water as evenly as they could with their giant squeegees.

On a true Zamboni, you will see the name "Zamboni" on the front of the machine. But don't be surprised if you see the word "Olympia" instead. That's the first competitor of the Zamboni. It is made in Canada.

Rink managers don't want skaters to keep skating after the announcer has asked everyone to clear the ice at the end of a session. The reason has to do with safety. The ice-resurfacing machine, which weighs almost 7000 pounds, cannot stop; it can only slow down as it slides on the ice. Remember that its rubber tires are moving on a slippery surface. Be considerate and safe by leaving the ice as quickly as possible when you are told.

The Zamboni Zone

Be careful as you skate past the corner where the Zamboni enters and leaves the ice. The surface will be rough in this area. Don't pick this spot to try a new move.

Zamboni Items You Can Buy

The Zamboni Company makes T-shirts, baseball caps, pins, key rings, belt buckles, and coffee mugs. They even have a car bumper sticker that reads, "My Other Car is a Zamboni." You can contact the company at: Zamboni, P.O. Box 770, Paramount, CA 90723 or at www.zamboni.com.

OTHER THINGS YOU SHOULD KNOW ABOUT SKATING RINKS

- Your rink will probably have a checkroom or rental lockers, or both, where you can leave your extra clothes and personal belongings while you skate. Sometimes skaters leave their shoes under a bench, but using a locker is always safer.

- Some rinks rent lockers for the whole season.

- At some rinks, you can bring your own lock and use an available locker. Elsewhere you will need quarters or other coins to operate the lockers.

- At an artificially frozen indoor rink you will not need to dress as warmly as you would at an outdoor rink.

- If your skating clothes don't have a pocket, use a safety pin to fasten your locker key on your clothing.

- Most rinks have schedules of public sessions as well as specialty sessions for hockey, figure skating, and ice dancing. Once you know the schedule at your rink, you can decide which kind of session is best for you. Many rinks change their schedules seasonally.

- Almost every rink has a snack bar, water fountain, public restrooms, and a comfortable waiting area for nonskaters.

WARM-UP EXERCISES

Now that you know what to expect at the rink, how to speak the language of skating, and how to overcome your fears, you are ready to skate. But before you step onto the ice, there is one more important thing for you to do: get warmed up.

You have probably played enough sports to know how important it is to warm up your body first before exercising. Warming up is even more important before ice skating because you are using your body in a room filled with cold, cold ice. This ice makes the air cold as well. Skaters have to take their warm-ups more seriously than other athletes.

As you know, the most important piece of equipment in skating is your body. The first step toward making this complicated machine work properly *on* the ice is to do warm-up exercises *off* the ice. Warm-up exercises have two functions: to avoid injuries and to decrease the time spent warming up on the ice. Most skaters are in a hurry to get on the ice. But it's still a good idea to warm up before skating. Luckily, it doesn't take long to get your blood flowing faster and limber up your muscles.

Mini Warm-Up

- Start with walking. If you come to your rink by car, get out of the vehicle at the far end of the parking lot. Walk briskly to the entrance.
- Before you lace up your skates, warm up your ankles by sitting on a bench or chair with one leg stretched out so that it is parallel to the floor. Rotate your ankle in circles, both directions. Do the same on the other ankle. You will

be amazed how much easier it is to bend your ankles when you warm them up first.

- After lacing your skates, walk to the rink entrance, but walk with your ankles and knees deeply bent. This looks funny, and it feels funny, too, but you'll feel the benefits. When other skaters catch on, they will join you in doing this deep-knee-bending walk.

To warm up the bending muscles of your skating side and the inner muscles of your free side:

- Stand on the rubber mat facing the railing. Place your feet about two feet apart.
- Bend deeply on one side, so that your bent knee is over your toe, and the other leg is stretched out. Feel the inner muscles of the free leg pulling slightly. If you can't feel a slight pull, bend more or separate the feet more.
- Do the same thing on the other side.
- Repeat this stretch from three to twelve times on each side.

Now you want to warm up your upper body and your back.

- Stretch your back by reaching up and lifting your torso away from your hips.
- Lower your arms until the fingertips are at hip level. With your legs stationary, twist your upper body (from the middle of the hips upward), pulling against your lower body (from the middle of the hips downward). Allow your arms and head to turn freely against your hips. You will feel a twist in your middle.

This mini warm-up takes very little time. The walk from the car to the rink warms up the hamstrings. The ankle exercise at the bench where you sit and lace your skates gets you ready for bending. The bent-knee walk lifts your torso and helps you bend your ankles and knees. Stretching at the railing, before you step on the ice, warms the muscles you'll use for stroking. The final side-to-side twist will loosen and warm up your upper body.

Now, I'll bet you're feeling ready to skate.

CHAPTER THREE

MOVING ON THE ICE

You have your skates; you've warmed up your body. You know about tracings, and you have a good understanding of fear and confidence. You are ready to step onto the slippery ice.

Make sure your blade guards are off as you hold the railing to steady yourself and bring both feet to the ice. No matter how good a skater you become, always hold the railing as you step onto (or off) the ice. Often this spot on the ice is rough, and people may be coming and going there, so you'll want to be extra careful. Still holding the railing, move away from the entrance to a less crowded spot.

The first thing you will do is to "feel" the ice through your blades. It is slippery! The slippery quality is what allows you to glide, but at the same time, it is what scares you. Let your feet slide back and forth as you hold the railing with both hands. Keep your ankles bent so that your center of gravity is close to the ice. Keep your weight over the center part of the blade. Don't let it go too far toward the back of the blade or toward the toe picks. The toe picks should not scratch the ice. Think of your blade as having three equal sections. In the beginning your weight should be over the middle third.

When you get used to the feeling of sliding, bring your feet together. Now pick up one foot at a time, and while holding onto the railing with both hands, try transferring the body weight from one blade to the other. Again, keep your ankles bent. After a while, you may feel a little foolish, because you're not yet gliding; you're kind of marching in place on the ice. This is all right. You are beginning to learn how to glide and skate with ease. You are also learning to keep your weight in the middle section of the blade.

As you feel more confident, stand sideways and see if you can do the same thing with only one hand on the railing. It is tempting to look down at your feet. Don't do it! Remember that your head is heavy, and if it is not in the correct position, you will be out of balance. Keep your chin level with the ice surface. Before you know it, you are taking steps and moving forward on the ice, with one hand loosely resting on the railing.

At this point, we can't really call this skating, but you will be gliding—and not holding on to the railing—on one foot very soon. As you move, be aware of the five points of posture: your head, the back, the arms, the skating leg (particularly the ankle), and your free leg.

- Your head should be level.
- Your back should be straight.
- Your arms should be out with your fingertips at hip level.
- Your skating ankle should be bent.
- Your free foot should be off the ice as you take steps. Eventually, your free leg will be extended out to the side of your body.

Of the five points of posture, only the free leg is not yet at its ultimate position (being fully extended). Right now, you simply want to balance on one foot at a time.

Bending before each step is a habit that you should establish right from the beginning. Always bend when transferring your weight from foot to foot, edge to edge, or direction to direction. The purpose of this bending is to get the center of gravity down, close to the ice, before the weight of the body is transferred, so that the new body position has a low center of gravity just as soon as possible. Keeping your weight low makes for smooth, effortless gliding.

The natural tendency for a nervous beginner is just the opposite of what skating teachers want. Nervous beginners' bodies become stiff. They have tension in their shoulders. Their shoulders, arms, and hands rise too high upward. The ankles and knees almost lock. Their weight goes over the front of their skates. Their toe picks scratch the ice. If this happens to you, you are not alone. It will take time to do just the opposite of what your body seems to want to do. Start by taking deep breaths. Transfer your weight to the new foot as you exhale. Take your time. The time you spend learning to move, *before* you learn to skate, is very worthwhile.

Learning to move on the ice by walking slowly and resting your hand on the railing can take from a few hours to a dozen or more practice sessions. Don't expect to learn more until you feel the five body positions and your center of gravity is low and over the middle third of the blade. When you are comfortable moving on the ice, you will be ready for the next step.

FALLING

Falling is part of learning and, unfortunately, part of performing. Beginners do it, and Olympic skaters do it, too. If you think of a fall as a slide, you will have less fear. Once you are beyond the point of no return, try to let your body *slide* to the ice. When your body tries to resist a fall, you are more at risk for an injury.

You can't really prepare for a fall because it happens so quickly. But there is a way to adjust yourself to the idea of falling. Late in the day, or when you are relaxed and ready to sleep, visualize yourself in a fall or slide. Picture yourself at a slow speed, a fast speed, and from all angles. Think of it neutrally, without fear or worry. This image will help you to respond with less tension when a fall actually happens. Your hands will automatically go out to protect your body in a fall. Because of this natural instinct, it is important to wear wrist guards. As your body goes with the direction of the fall, you will find yourself sliding on one hip, with your hands on the ice.

The general rule of etiquette at rinks is that when you fall, you should get up quickly—for your safety and for the safety of others. If you are hurt, and you don't get up right away, other skaters will ask if you need help. Rinks usually have first-aid supplies and employees who are trained to help. Most falls don't result in any serious injuries. You may have a bruise or sore spot for a few days. But sometimes a serious fall can cause a concussion, broken bone, or sprain. Knowing how to fall and having the right equipment will help you avoid injury.

Falls don't mean you are a poor skater. Some top skaters fall often, and some beginners never fall. Often falls occur because you or another skater are trying to avoid a collision. Accept the fact that you will sometimes fall, and when it happens try to go with the flow. If you are not hurt, get up and try the skating move again.

GETTING UP FROM A FALL

When you see skaters fall in competition on television, they get back up so fast they look almost like bouncing Ping-Pong balls. There are two reasons for this: one, skaters are trained to get up quickly; and two, they want the fall to be the smallest part of their program. If a program is four minutes, and a fall is five seconds, that means the fall is only about two percent of the total program. For your safety and that of other skaters you should get up quickly.

- Assuming you are not hurt, first get in a kneeling position on the ice. Bring one foot forward with your arms on both

Getting up from a fall: two positions

sides of the bent leg. Your hands will be on both sides of your foot.

The next step is the most important: the leg and foot that are behind you have an important function. The toe picks of that blade will stab the ice. If the toe picks are not in the ice, you are likely to slip and fall as you are getting up.

It helps a lot to understand how your blade is designed. When the toe picks are in the ice, the blade can't move. If the toe picks clear the ice surface, you can move either forward or backward.

- With the toe picks of the back foot in the ice, press your weight forward onto your two hands, on either side of your forward foot.
- Slowly straighten up. As your arms go out for balance, keep your ankles bent, and your back straight.
- Slowly rise up. Take your time, constantly feeling your balance over your blades.

Falling and getting up from a fall are great exercises for warming up the body. Many different muscles are used, and you are picking up your own body weight (weight lifting) and stretching a number of muscles all at once.

Forward Swizzles

This movement has many names. "Swizzles" is the common name in the eastern United States, but it is also called Wiggles, Sculls, Paragraphs, and even Lemons. Actually, the word "lemons" best describes their shape.

> ### Are you ready to swizzle?
>
> Before learning to do forward swizzles, make sure you can stand upright on your skates and bend your knees with a straight back.

Swizzles are done on two feet. Their purpose is to make you aware of the power you have when your body is in the correct position. This move is the beginning of skating without holding the railing. You will enjoy your first experience of gliding.

You will be coordinating two movements. One is the basic movement in skating: bending the ankles. The other is a rhythmic movement of turning the ankles in—as in a pigeon-toed position—and out—in a "Charlie Chaplin position."

- Start close to the railing, so you can hold on with an outstretched arm.
- Check that your ankles are bent, your knees are over your toes, your back is straight, your arms are out, and your chin is level with the ice.
- Bend more, so that you feel your two inner edges grip the ice.
- Allow this grip to press your feet outward. They will slide forward, making a curved shape.

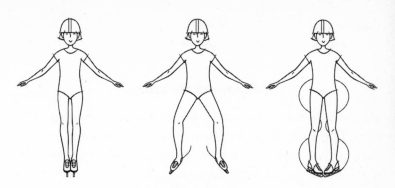

Swizzle: three positions

At this point, two things happen. Your ankles will start to unbend, and you will turn your toes in toward each other. Let your toes come together, but not close enough to touch.

Now you have completed one swizzle. You caused your body to move over the ice, making a pair of tracings that look something like parentheses. What the blade does on the ice is the result of your body position and the way you change positions.

- Using the momentum from your first swizzle, repeat the process to do more swizzles. The successive swizzles are easier because you are not starting from a standstill.

As you do this exercise, gradually let go of the railing and move away, until you are about eight feet from it. Achieving independence from the railing is an important step. Congratulate yourself!

Being this far from the railing means that, if you fall, you will not hurt yourself by hitting it. In addition, these eight feet of independence give you a feeling of confidence because you are now moving on your own. The distance also allows you to keep your arms out, assisting your balance.

Continue practicing your swizzles with a straight back, staying about eight feet away from the railing. From the top of your head to your hips, your body is in the same position that it will be in for the next step: forward skating one foot at a time.

FORWARD SKATING

Forward skating is also called forward stroking. The most basic step of figure skating, it can be done correctly in many different ways. If you spoke to ten coaches, they would probably have ten different ways to teach forward skating. Some coaches teach it one way to beginners, and another way to more advanced skaters. The one thing all teachers agree on is that the power is gained from pushing from the inside of the edge.

Never push from the toe! Pushing from the toe is a sure sign of a self-taught skater. It is probably the most difficult bad habit for coaches to correct. The reason skaters do it is it seems to work. Pushing against the toe gives the skater the false feeling of a good grip against the ice.

The trouble is, when you push against the toe, the top of your body has to bend over to get this grip. Then, when you've gotten this incorrect push, your body starts to straighten up. As that happens, your speed decreases. So there is no benefit in the long run. Don't push with your toe. It's not worth it, and it is a hard habit to break.

Are you ready for forward skating?

Before you learn forward skating, make sure you are comfortable doing swizzles. You should be able to do them smoothly and with a consistent speed.

OCCASIONAL
SKATERS

The right way to push starting from a stand still position

- Place your feet in a "V" position. Your heels should be together, and your toes should be apart. Make sure that your head is level, your back is straight, and your arms are out with your fingertips at hip level.

- Bend both ankles as you shift your weight to the inside edge of the right blade.

This starting position will allow you to grip the ice with your right inside edge as you transfer your weight to glide forward on your left foot. On this first stroke your left blade will be balancing on the inside edge. As a beginner, try to stay balanced on one foot for a count of two beats before you change to the other foot. Eventually you'll be balancing for six beats on each stroke.

- As you glide on one foot, unbend your skating ankle slightly as you bring your free foot in next to the skating foot. Before you transfer your weight to the new foot, bend more so that you are on a deeper inside edge as you press against the gripping edge. The gripping edge is the end of the last edge you were on. The sooner you establish the habit of bending before you transfer to a new edge, foot or direction, the faster you will make progress.

If you find yourself struggling to keep your skating direction straight, it is probably because your shoulders are swinging as you change from one foot to another. Swinging your shoulders is correct when you're walking, but not in forward skating. To avoid this common problem, concentrate on looking straight ahead. Focus on an imaginary spot straight ahead of you. Imagine that point being one tip of a triangle; the opposite side of the triangle will be your shoulder line. In this way you will be much more in control of your hips, shoulders, and arms. Make

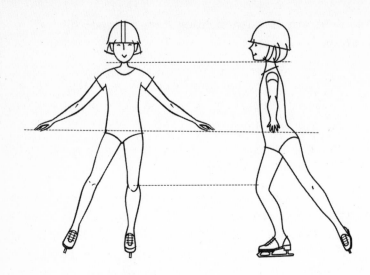

Forward skating

Head level
Back straight
Arms out, fingertips at hip level
Skating leg bent at the knee and the ankle
Free leg extended, free foot off the ice

sure you are not holding your arms too high. If your arms are too high, your shoulders will be too high, your center of gravity will be too high, and you will lose control of the edge.

As you become more comfortable with your forward skating, be aware of your body position at the critical time of changing feet. Don't lean forward at this point; think of your torso and hips as one unit. Do not break at the waist.

- When your feet come together, the new foot will be placed slightly ahead of the foot from which you are pushing. The faster your speed over the ice, the farther ahead the new foot will go.

  Each stroke will get its power from pushing against the inside edge of the last stroke. The new stroke will be on a slight inside edge.

You will develop a rhythm to these strokes as your balance becomes consistent.

• As you approach the first corner of your rink, glide on both feet with your ankles bent and your right arm forward and across your body. Although you are on two feet, your weight will be mostly on your left foot and you will feel it on the outside edge of your left foot. Later, when you feel more confident, you will use forward crossovers instead of this two-footed glide at the corners of your rink. But for now, the two-foot position is a safe way to go around the curve.

• As your speed slows, bring your right arm back to the side of your body (the three o'clock position) as you resume forward skating. When you reach the next corner of the rink, repeat the two-foot glide with your right arm forward and across your body.

• As you continue to skate around the rink, hold the balance on one foot for as long as you can.

Is one foot stronger than the other?

As you work on balancing on one foot, you might discover that you are stronger on one foot than the other. If that happens to you, don't worry. It is common. With practice, you will grow stronger on the weaker side.

• Make sure that you are bending enough before you transfer the balance to the "weak" foot.

• If you are sure you are bending equally, make sure that you are not "popping up" in your skating ankle and knee once your weight is on the new foot.

If one leg is stronger than the other, try this exercise:

Let's say your left side is weaker.

- Start forward skating on the left foot, but instead of timing each stroke the same way, count to three for the left (weaker) foot, and one for the right (stronger) side.

- Skate around the rink with this uneven timing. The exercise will strengthen the muscles on the weak side. It will also make you aware of the importance of bending before you transfer your weight, and of not popping up once the weight is on the new foot. Uneven balance in skating is called limping. By doing this exercise, you will have evenly timed forward skating.

THE SNOWPLOW STOP

If you were riding a new bicycle, you would want to know how to use the brakes. In skating, it is also important to know how to stop. There are several different stops in skating. All of them involve scraping the ice surface to come to a complete stop.

How to snowplow

- Stand in a "T" position, with your right heel against your left instep.
- Bend both knees (1) and push on to your right foot, then onto your left.
- You have taken two forward strokes and you have a bit of speed.
- Your arms should be out to your sides.
- Glide with your weight equally divided on both feet. Your knees and ankles should be deeply bent.
- Move your arms forward from your sides and stretch them out in front of you. Keep your arms low so that your fin-

gertips are still at your hip line (about where a jacket ends). (2)

- Shift your weight onto your right foot.

- Keep both blades flat so that all four edges are on the ice.

- Don't allow your ankles to turn in.

- Scrape your right foot across the ice out to your right side, but slightly ahead of the left foot. (3)

- When you feel and hear the scrape, you know you are doing the snowplow correctly.

- Apply more pressure to the right blade, which is scraping both edges against the ice.

In your final position, you will have both knees bent.

- The right foot will be ahead of the left and will be turned toward the left (very pigeon-toed).

- The left foot will be pointing straight ahead.

- Most of your weight will be on your right foot.

- Your feet will be about eighteen inches apart.

- Both arms will still be forward, straight out in front of your body.

Skating direction   Start

Snowplow stop

In your figure skating, you will learn different stops. The basic stops are all the same in one respect: they all involve scraping the ice with your blade. Mastering the snowplow stop will make it easier for you to learn the other stops.

Tip: A common mistake is to do a good snowplow stop, but then drop your head down to look at your feet. Keep your head and eyes up and look straight ahead. This position gives you better balance, and it makes you feel what you are doing. Training yourself to feel what you are doing is important in learning.

FORWARD CROSSOVERS

Forward crossovers will be your first experience of leaning on an edge. Forward crossovers are done one foot at a time and one edge at a time. We'll first do crossovers in a counterclockwise direction, since that is the usual direction of skating in a rink.

- Start in a "T" position with your left heel at your right instep.
- The upper part of your body will be turned toward the left, facing point A in the illustration. Hold this position throughout the crossovers.
- Bending both knees, push onto your left forward outside edge.
- Extend your free foot (right) straight outside the circle shape while bending well in your skating knee. (2)
- Now, bring your right foot and cross it over your left foot, placing it onto the ice on a right inside edge. At the same time, feel the push from your left outside edge as it pushes toward the right side of your body. Stay down in your knees and don't lift the right foot any higher than necessary since lifting it too high can disturb your center of gravity. (3)

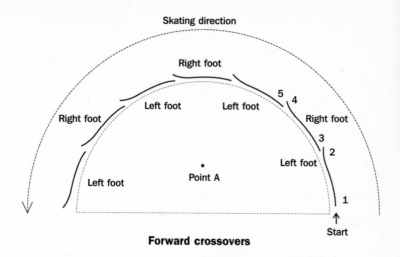

Forward crossovers

- While on your right inside edge, keep your skating knee bent while you extend your free foot straight outside the circle shape. (4)

- Repeat to practice successive crossovers.

- Practice the opposite direction.

- Everyone has a natural sense of rotation, as well as a strong and weak foot for balancing. Practice more in the weaker direction than the stronger direction.

If your rink has a mirror, you might be surprised to observe the good lean of your body. You may not, at first, believe that it is you. The lean comes from being in the correct position and

---

Practicing Crossovers

To perfect your crossovers, practice them with different-sized circles. Start on a small circle, and gradually make your circles larger and larger, much like a coil.

having sufficient speed over the ice. If you try to lean, it doesn't work. Concentrate on the five posture points and bend well in your ankles, so that each stroke renews your speed over the ice, and you'll have the lean.

Crossovers are the beginning of edges, and edges are the beginning of figure skating. Congratulate yourself—you have reached an important milestone.

Are you ready for swing rolls?

Before learning outside and inside swing rolls, you should be able to balance easily for six beats on each foot in your forward skating.

FORWARD OUTSIDE SWING ROLLS

When you skate on an edge, you are making a curved tracing on the ice. If you stay on the edge long enough, you will make a circle, coming back to the place where you started. A circle is one-half of a figure eight. In figure skating, most of your moves will not form a complete circle. Most moves are done on curves that you can picture as a part of a circle. The next move you are going to do draws a half-circle on the ice. The swing roll is a half-circle done on one foot then the other.

Each half-circle—or lobe, as it is often called—is divided into three parts.

- The first third is where you have the most power from your pushoff.

- The second third is where you change the position of your free foot and your arms.

OCCASIONAL
SKATERS

> ### Swing rolls help to develop your thigh muscles.
>
> Don't be surprised if your legs feel tired after doing swing rolls. You are using your thigh muscles more than in any move you have done so far.

- The last third is where you need to have enough flow to ride your edge and bend to do your pushoff into the next half-circle.

The distance between pushoffs should be at least equal to your height, but not more than three times your height. In the beginning, your half-circles will be small, but as you practice the pushoff you will gain more power, and the half-circles will become larger.

Doing outside swing rolls

- Start in the "T" position with your right heel at your left instep.
- Your upper body should be turned, so that your right arm and shoulder are forward and over the future tracing.
- Your left arm should be to your side, with the left shoulder relaxed.

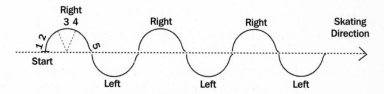

Forward outside swing rolls

- Keep your head and eyes looking ahead on your half circle. (1)
- Bend both knees and push off onto your right outside edge.
- Extend your left leg behind, so that your left foot is over your tracing. This extension stabilizes the first third of the half-circle. Your arms and shoulders haven't yet moved. (2)
- At the beginning of the second third, your free foot will come from behind to in front, over the future tracing. (3) If you bring your left knee into your right leg, then bring your free foot forward, you will be able to avoid the common problem of over-rotation. Before the end of the second third, your arms and shoulders should rotate to your right so that your left arm moves forward, over your future tracing. Your right arm will be to your right side, and your right shoulder will be relaxed. (4)
- On the last third, ride in this position until the pushoff.
- Keep your free foot in front, with your ankle turned out slightly and your toe pointing down. Your arms and shoulders should remain where they are, left arm over the tracing and right arm out to your right side.
- Just before the end of the half-circle, pivot your skating foot to your right, as you bring the heel of your left foot to the instep of your right foot.
- Bend deeply in both knees (5) as you transfer your weight to the new foot for the left forward outside swing roll.
- Repeat these steps as you perform your next swing roll. Your deepest knee bend should always be just before your push-off. Keep this deep knee bend into the second third of the new swing roll.

When you do swing rolls well, you will make a neat tracing of symmetrical semicircles on the ice. You will also feel the rhythm of bending at each pushoff, moving the arms and shoulders in a controlled manner, and moving the free foot from back to front.

FORWARD INSIDE SWING ROLLS

Forward inside swing rolls make a series of half-circles on the ice, just like the tracings of the outside swing roll. But this time, instead of skating on the forward outside edge, you will use the forward inside edge.

Once again, each half-circle, or lobe, is divided into three parts.

- In the first third, you have the most power from your pushoff.

- In the second third, you change the position of your free foot and your arms.

- In the last third you ride your edge and do your pivot pushoff into the next half-circle.

Sound familiar? You're right. Forward outside and inside swing rolls call on many of the same skills.

Doing inside swing rolls

- Start in the "T" position with your right heel at your left instep. Your upper body will be turned so that your left arm and shoulder will be forward and over the future tracing. Your right arm will be to your right side, with your

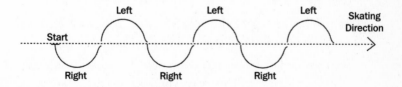

Forward inside swing rolls

Having problems with swing rolls?

- Ask yourself where and why you are losing control.

- During the first third, if you are "popping" up in your skating knee, your bending muscles may not be as strong as they need to be. Go back to working on your forward swizzles. See how slowly you can come up in the knees.

- On the second third of the lobe, if your arms are rotating too far in the direction of your lobe, it could be for one of two basic reasons: your arms could be too high, or your free side could be rotating too much. The higher the arms are, the higher your center of gravity will be, and the less control you'll have. Try to relax both shoulders and arms. Remember, fingertips should be at hip level.

right shoulder relaxed. Keep your head and eyes looking ahead on your half-circle.

- As you bend both knees to push off onto your right inside edge, extend your left leg behind so that your left foot is over your tracing. This extension stabilizes the first third of the half-circle.

- Your arms and shoulders should remain in the same position as when you started—left arm forward, right arm to your right side.

- At the beginning of the second third, your free foot will come from behind to front, over the future tracing.

- Bring your left knee into your right leg, then bring your free foot forward. This way, you can avoid the common problem of over-rotation.

- Before the end of the second third, your arms and shoulders should rotate to your left so that your right arm will now be forward over your future tracing, your left arm should be to your left side, and your left shoulder should be relaxed.

- On the last third, ride in this position until the pushoff.

- Keep your free foot in front, with your ankle turned out slightly and your toe pointing down.

- Keep your arms and shoulders where they are—right arm over the tracing and left arm out to your left side.

- Just before the end of the half-circle, pivot your skating foot to your right as you bring the heel of your left foot to the instep of your right foot.

- Bend deeply in both knees as you transfer your weight to the new foot for the left forward inside swing roll.

- Repeat these steps as you perform your next swing roll on your left inside edge. Your deepest knee bend is always just before your pushoff, and you should hold this deep knee bend into the second third of the next swing roll.

The Power of Swing Rolls

Swing rolls give you great training for controlled knee bending and feeling the total lean of the body. The more speed you have, the deeper the lean of the body will be. Swing rolls will help you become more comfortable with leaning on your edges.

GAMES FOR FORWARD SKATING

If you have trouble with your forward skating, it is probably because you aren't bending enough. Try these games and see if your bending improves.

"Under the Pole"

Here's a good game for a group to play on the ice. Have two adults hold the ends of a long pole. The skaters line up, and one at a time, each takes several strokes. Gliding on two feet, they skate under the pole. The adults gradually lower the pole to make it more challenging. The lower the pole, the more you have to bend your knees and ankles to go under it.

"Through the Tunnel"

If only one adult is available, the pole can be placed touching the railing horizontally. The adult stands as far away as he or she can and holds the pole horizontal, as the students go under it. As the pole is lowered, the skaters have to bend more to go under it.

Game: "Through the Tunnel"

"Bend on the Line"

Another way of practicing bending is to have students skate from one side of the rink to the other. About twenty feet before the far side, draw a line parallel to the end railing (this can be done with a magic marker, the heel of one blade, or a scraping mark). When the skaters reach this line, that is their cue to bend their ankles and knees as they glide in a bent position.

These bending games can help you gain confidence to do the skating moves you are learning. Of course, you may be successful at bending your ankles and knees, but you may not have good posture in your upper body. If that happens, think of bending while sliding down a wall. Remember to keep your head level, with your eyes looking ahead and your chin level with the ice.

CHAPTER FOUR

MOVING BACKWARD

Skating backward is cool! When skaters sign up for skating classes, they often say that they just want to learn basics up to and including backward skating. There is something about seeing someone skate backward that makes you think, "Boy, that's something I could do." That's right, but learning it takes a little patience.

Correct backward skating is faster than correct forward skating for two reasons: (1) When skating backward, the weight is on the middle third of the blade as it is in forward skating, but it is even farther forward, where there is less friction between the blade and the ice; (2) the back is ever so slightly pitched forward for better air dynamics.

Just as we began with forward swizzles as the way to learn to skate forward, we'll start with back swizzles as the best way to learn to skate backward.

Are you ready for back swizzles?

Stand facing the railing. Bend your knees. Use your hands to push yourself backward gently. If you are comfortable gliding backward for a couple of feet, you are ready to learn back swizzles.

OCCASIONAL SKATERS

Tip: You might see skaters going backward by wiggling their backsides. This kind of motion is okay for hockey skaters, but not for figure skaters. In backward skating, as in forward skating, keep your back straight and get your power from bending your knees and ankles.

BACK SWIZZLES

- Face the railing of the rink, with both feet in a pigeon-toed position.
- Bend your ankles and feel both of your inside edges grip the ice.
- With a little push from the railing to give you momentum, allow your feet to separate as they go out to your sides.
- Your arms should be slightly forward, and your elbows relaxed.
- Your feet shouldn't go farther apart than the distance between your elbows. When feet separate to the widest point of the swizzle, reverse the bending process as you pull up in the knees and feel the inside edges pulling in toward one another. Your feet will pass through a position of being side-by-side, toes straight ahead. You have completed one back swizzle.
- Pivot your feet, to a pigeon-toed position, to start your second swizzle.

Swizzles are a great way to move backward from one spot to another. But they also have another benefit. Practicing swizzles helps build strength in the muscles of the insides of your legs. The stronger these muscles are, the more power you will have when you are extending your free foot, because the free foot is dependent on these inside leg muscles.

You will develop a rhythm as you learn to coordinate the moves of the backward swizzles:

- Pivot the feet.
- Grip the inside edges.
- Bend.
- Come up in the knees.
- Pull in inside edges together.
- Repeat.

When you practice your backward swizzles, check your tracings. The two curved lines should mirror each other. Your aims are to have equal-sized tracings, and to go in a straight axis from your starting point. If your tracings are uneven, one side has more power and control than the other. If your axis points toward one side, then one side is stronger than the other.

> **Tip:** Before learning back skating, make sure your back swizzles are comfortable and done at a good speed.

BACK SKATING (ON ONE FOOT AT A TIME)

Back skating, like forward skating, can be done in different ways, but using the back inside edges to push and to glide on is the easiest way to begin.

- Start by facing the railing and holding on with both hands.
- With your feet together, bend both ankles.
- Pick up your right foot and place it to your right side, about a foot away.

- As you transfer your weight to your right foot, pick up your left foot and bring it off the ice, touching the inside of your right ankle.
- Bend both ankles and repeat this motion to the left.

You will be stepping from side to side, balancing on one foot at a time. Make sure you always bend well in your ankles before you step to the side. Continue doing this step, from side to side, until it is automatic. When you don't have to think about what you are doing, you are ready to add another motion to the move.

Besides stepping from side to side, make sure you always step on the inside edge of the blade. This is important because in a little while, when you push away from the railing, you will be shifting onto the other foot as you push against the inside edge of the blade you are leaving.

- Continue stepping with a bent ankle from side to side on the inside edges, until it is automatic.
- Before your weight shifts from one foot to another, turn the new foot in, in a pigeon-toed position. Now, the new foot will not only be on an inside edge, but the direction of the blade will be ready to start a curved, back inside edge.

Make sure that no skaters are behind you, as they wouldn't be expecting you to push off into their track. When you are on your left foot, give a light push away from the railing at the same

Tip: The most difficult part of backward skating is starting. Like many moves in figure skating, once you have momentum, the move falls into place. If you lose your momentum, simply go back to the railing and start all over again.

> **Tip:** When you are skating backward, you are responsible for looking where you are going. Every third step, turn your head to see if the coast is clear.

time that you shift your weight onto your right foot. You will glide backward on your right back inside edge.

- As soon as you feel this gliding motion, bend your right ankle, and step to your left side, just as you did when you were holding on to the railing.
- Keep both arms slightly relaxed at the elbows.
- Continue to transfer the weight from one inside edge to another, always bending well in your ankle.

You are trying to balance on one foot at a time for a beat of three—count "one <u>and</u> two <u>and</u> three." Saying the word "and" in between the numbers will create consistency in your counting.

BACK STOPPING

Guess what? Backstopping is easier to do than forward stopping. You don't have to turn in your toes in a pigeon-toe position.

Start by doing your back skating from a light push from the railing. When you have enough speed to test how this easy backstop works, you'll do three things:

1. Bend both ankles.
2. Bring your arms from the side of your body to the front of your body.
3. Press both feet on all edges out to the sides of your body.

If your ankles were bent, and not favoring either the inside or the outside edge, you scraped the flat part of each blade against the ice, making a full stop backward.

Once you feel confident about your backward stop, your backward skating will improve. Now you know how to get out of those backward moves when your speed increases. You have a feeling of security, knowing that you can stop.

Are You Ready for Back Crossovers?

Before learning back crossovers, make sure you can hold your backward skating at least three beats on each foot.

BACK CROSSOVERS

This basic backward move combines the skills of two things you already have learned: back skating on one foot at a time, and forward crossovers. Back crossovers are the fastest way of skating from one point to another. Without them, advanced skaters wouldn't gain enough speed for their multi-rotation jumps. If you've watched figure skating, you know how smooth and powerful back crossovers are. Olympians have been clocked at twenty miles per hour. Back crossovers require patience. Be prepared to start off very jerkily and slowly. Take it one step at a time, literally.

You will learn the back crossovers in a counterclockwise direction first. Back crossovers are similar to forward crossovers, except for the actual crossover. In the forward crossovers, you are on one foot at a time, always pushing from an edge. In the back crossovers there are two parts. For the first part of the move, you are balancing on two feet, and for the next part, you are balancing on one back inside edge.

- Start with your feet pointing inward ("pigeon-toed") and do two back swizzles. They will give you the necessary

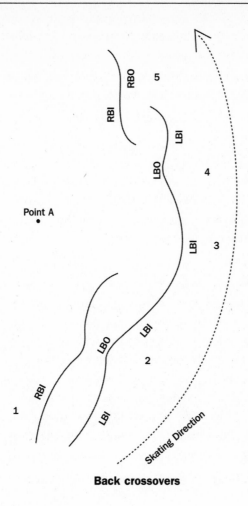

Back crossovers

speed to do your back crossovers. Do your backward swizzles in a curved line, not straight back. Your weight will be mostly on your right foot. (1)

- At the end of the second swizzle, turn your upper body into point A. Your left shoulder will be pressed forward. Your head will be turned so that your eyes will be looking over your right shoulder, in the direction you are going. (2)

- Transfer your weight entirely to your right foot by lifting your left foot up and then over your right foot.

- Stay down in your knees so that you feel a push against your right back outside edge as you transfer your weight. (3)

- Now, on your left back inside edge, stay down in your skating knee as you extend your free leg behind your left leg and straight outside the circle shape. (4)

- Hold this edge for three slow beats. Count one and two and three for a consistent rhythm.

- Repeat from the end of the second swizzle by stepping beside on your right edge. (5)

Crossovers should be beautiful and smooth. The toe picks should not scratch the ice. If you are scratching the toe of your right foot, it is probably because you are picking up that foot too soon. If you are scratching the toe of your left foot, it is usually because you are leaning forward, with your backside out.

Practice your crossovers both counterclockwise, as described above, and clockwise. You will use both directions to prepare for your jumps and spins. When you have mastered back crossovers, and you want to increase your speed, do as described, but keep your left blade on the ice when going counterclockwise.

GAMES FOR BACKWARD SKATING

"The Partner Game"

At one width end of the rink, have two skaters face one another and hold hands. One skater skates backward and the other skates forward until they reach the middle of the rink. There, they switch positions and continue to the other width end of the rink.

To switch positions, the skater going forward does a forward snowplow stop. The partner (the skater going backward) does a

Tip: The skater going forward is responsible for not bumping into other skaters; he or she can see where they both are going. The skater skating backwards is responsible for deciding the speed. Both skaters will bend their knees and ankles, yet keep their backs straight. All it takes is one of the skaters leaning forward to pull both skaters down.

backward stop. Then both skaters sidestep around so that the one who was going backward is now going forward.

"Crossovers in a Circle"

This game is done with a group of skaters. Make a circle, hold hands, and face the center of the circle. Then, while keeping this grip, everyone should take tiny steps backward. The increased distance makes a larger circle, and more important, a rounder circle, as arms and hands will be stretched out.

To practice back crossovers in a counterclockwise direction:

- Skaters continue to hold hands.
- With feet together, all turn ninety degrees to their left (a counterclockwise turn).
- Still holding hands, all bend (to start a back swizzle), with most of the weight over the right foot. Each skater picks up the left foot and crosses it over the right foot.
- Balance on the left foot, and repeat.
- Practice in the opposite direction as well.

Back Skating in a Straight Line

Another good way to practice back-skating moves is to have a line of skaters all face the end of the rink, with their hands on each others' shoulders. The line starts moving backward from one end of the rink. Moving together, all skaters in line do their best backward skating. They then see how far they can go as a line before the line breaks apart.

This game usually ends in laughter, which makes it almost impossible to maintain a straight back, but it's a great way to learn good posture and speed while practicing with friends.

CHAPTER FIVE

Turns and Spins

You are about to reach a level in skating that is really special. Your practice sessions won't feel like exercise drills anymore. You'll be combining the different moves that you've learned into patterns that you design. This is the beginning of choreography on ice.

Are you ready to learn to turn from skating forward to skating backward?

To learn turns, you should be able to skate comfortably, both forward and backward. You should be able to skate on your inside and outside edges with control and at a good speed.

The "33" Turn

The first turn you will learn is called the "33" turn. You'll see why shortly. It is a turn, from skating forward to backward, in a counterclockwise direction, done on two feet. You will skate on an imaginary circle. This move will be the basis for learning more advanced one-foot turns.

We'll start with a left 33 turn. Stand in a "T" position with your left heel at your right instep. Your right arm will be across your body and your right shoulder will be slightly forward. Your

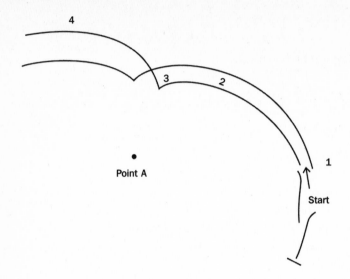

The 33 turn

left arm and shoulder will be behind. Your eyes will always look ahead on your circle.

- Take two strokes for speed—one on your right foot, then one on your left.

- Glide on both feet, with both knees bent and most of your weight on your left foot. (1)

- Rotate your arms into your circle, so that your right shoulder is toward point A. Keep your weight mostly on your left foot and your eyes looking ahead on the circle. (2)

To turn from forward to backward,

- Bend more deeply into your knees so that your weight is over the balls of both feet. The ball of your foot is the pivot point of your balance for turning.

- Keep most of your weight on your left foot as you turn into the circle shape from forward to backward.

- As you turn, your arms and shoulders will switch. Your right arm and shoulder, which were in front, will be behind you. Your left arm and shoulder, which were behind, will be in front of your body.
- Exit the turn with your left shoulder toward point A. (4)

When you turn from forward to backward while walking, your head also turns. In skating it's different: Your head will not turn. You will continue looking ahead on the circle throughout the entrance to the turn, the turn itself and the exit of the turn.

Hold the exit edge as long as the distance of your entrance edge.

- Stop by bending your knees and sliding the feet apart, just as you did in your first back stop. Now you can take a moment to admire the tracings of your first 33 turn, also called a "3" turn on two feet.

Look at your tracing and you will see two marks that look a lot like the number thirty-three.

Are you ready for the back outside Mohawk turn?

Before you can learn the backward Mohawk, your back swizzles and your skating must have control and speed.

BACK OUTSIDE MOHAWK TURN

Of the four basic Mohawk turns, the easiest ones to learn are the back Mohawks. These are entered on a back skating edge. All Mohawks are done from one direction to another, and from one edge to the same edge, on the other foot. Start with the right back outside to the left forward outside Mohawk.

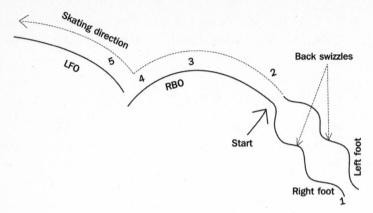

Back outside Mohawk

Backward Outside Mohawk

- Start on two feet with your toes close together. Your left arm and shoulder should be slightly forward and across your body. (1)
- Do two back swizzles in a counterclockwise direction to gain some speed.
- Glide on two feet.
- Lift up your left foot and extend it in front so you are balancing only on your right back outside edge with your free foot extended in front of your body (2).
- Rotate your arms to your left. As you do this you will be looking over your left shoulder to the outside of your circle shape. (3)
- Bring your left heel to the instep of your right foot. Turn it out to your left, the direction you are going. (4)
- The angle of the feet must be just a bit more than ninety degrees. Keep looking over your left shoulder in the direction you are skating.

- To turn from backward to forward, bend your knees more deeply as you transfer your weight from your right to left foot.

- As you turn, your arms and shoulders will switch, and you will exit the turn with your left shoulder and arm forward and across your body. (5)

- Extend your free foot behind and over your tracing.

- Holding the exit edge at least as long as your entrance edge, do a snowplow stop.

You've done your first Mohawk—a back outside Mohawk.

Are you ready to learn the forward Mohawk?

Make sure you can balance well in both your forward and back skating.

FORWARD INSIDE MOHAWK TURN

There are three ways to go from forward to backward: You can turn on two feet, a "33" turn; on one foot, a "three" turn; or you can go from one foot on a forward edge to your other foot on a backward edge. This third way of turning is called a forward Mohawk. This Mohawk is from right forward inside to left back inside.

- Start in a "T" position with your right heel at your left instep. Your right arm will be across your body, and your right shoulder will be slightly forward. Your left arm and shoulder will be behind. Keep your eyes ahead, on your circle shape.

OCCASIONAL SKATERS

> **Tip:** Here's a helpful general rule in figure skating: Any time you're changing direction, changing feet, or changing an edge, bend both your ankles deeply. Make this deep bend automatic just as soon as possible!

- Bend both knees and both ankles as you push onto your right forward inside edge. (1)
- Extend your free left foot behind you, over the tracing, for stability after your pushoff.
- Bring the heel of your free foot to the instep of your skating foot (be sure to turn your free foot toward the direction you came from).
- The angle of your feet should be more than ninety degrees.
- Rotate your arms into your circle shape so that your right shoulder is pressed toward point A. (2)
- To turn from forward to backward, keep your right shoulder pressed toward point A as you give a deeper bend into your knees and transfer your weight to your left back inside edge. (3)
- As you turn from forward to backward, your arms and shoulders will switch positions.
- Exit the turn with your left shoulder pressed toward point A. (4)
- Extend your free foot over your future tracing.
- Your head will be turned to your right, eyes looking where you are going.
- Hold the exit edge at least as long as the entrance edge.
- Put your free foot down on the ice to stop.

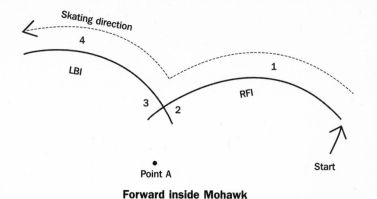

Forward inside Mohawk

You have performed a forward outside Mohawk—good work!

Are you ready to learn the three turn?

To do this turn, you will need to be able to skate forward and backward with good speed, and exit your Forward Mohawk with control.

FORWARD OUTSIDE THREE TURN

The forward outside three turn is like the Mohawk: You enter forward and exit backward. In the Mohawk you do the turn by changing from one foot to the other. In the three turn you go from forward to backward on one foot.

- Start in a "T" position with your left heel at your right instep. Your right arm should be across your body, and your right shoulder should be slightly forward. Your left arm and shoulder should be behind. Keep your eyes looking ahead on your circle shape.

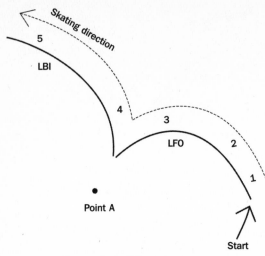

Forward outside three turn

- Bend both knees and both ankles as you push onto your left forward outside edge. (1)

- Extend your free foot behind you, over the tracing, for stability after your pushoff.

- Bring your right knee to the side of your skating leg (this keeps the hips stable). (2)

- As you rotate your arms into your circle, your right shoulder is pressed toward point A.

- Keep your eyes looking ahead on your circle.

- To turn from forward to backward, bend more deeply into your knee so that your weight is over the ball of your foot, the pivot point of your blade. (3)

- As you turn from forward to backward on your left foot, your arms and shoulders will switch positions. You will exit the turn with your left shoulder pressed toward point A, your free foot extended over the future tracing and your head and eyes looking ahead on your circle. (4)

> **Tip:** When you do a three turn, both the entrance and the exit are done on an imaginary circle with a diameter about equal to your height. The maneuver should take up at least half the circle. You will be working toward using the whole circle for the turn including the exit.

- After holding the exit edge at least as long as your entrance edge, put your free foot down to stop, and admire your tracing of your first three turn. (5) Super turn!
- You will see that your tracing resembles the number three.
- As you work on your three turns, you'll find that the turn itself isn't difficult, it's holding that back inside edge that's the tough job.
- Start on a RFO to do the RFO-RBI three turn.

Practice both three turns on larger and larger circles. Aim for a circle about three times your height in diameter.

> ### *Are you ready to learn waltzing on ice?*
>
> To learn this beautiful series of moves, you must have control of your forward outside-to-inside three turn, your back skating, and your backward Mohawk.

WALTZING

You can now combine the skating skills you've learned into a series of connecting moves. This is where the fun begins.

Three of the moves you've learned earlier are the LFO three turn, RBO backward Mohawk and the LFO edge with the free

OCCASIONAL
SKATERS

> **Tip:** Waltzing can be done in a half-circle pattern, a figure-eight pattern, and in an ice dance, like the American Waltz.

foot that swings forward. When you do the first two—an outside three turn and a step beside—that's called a waltz step. And when you put all three moves together, it's called waltzing.

Start in the middle of the rink for some waltzing.

- Start in your "T" position with your left heel at your right instep. Your right arm should be across your body, and your right shoulder should be slightly forward. Your left arm and shoulder should be behind. Keep your eyes looking ahead on your circle shape. (1)

- Push onto your left forward outside edge and extend your free foot behind, over your tracing.

- To do your forward three turn, rotate your arms and shoulders into your circle, so that your right shoulder is closest to point A.

- Bend more deeply into your left knee so that you are over the pivot point of the blade. (2)

- Keep looking ahead on the circle shape as you turn from forward to backward and switch positions of your arms and shoulders. (3)

- On your exit, your left shoulder is pressed toward point A.

- Extend your free foot over the future tracing. (4) The next move is the right back outside edge.

- Bring your right foot in next to your left. (5)

- Bend both knees and push against your left back inside edge on to your right back outside edge.

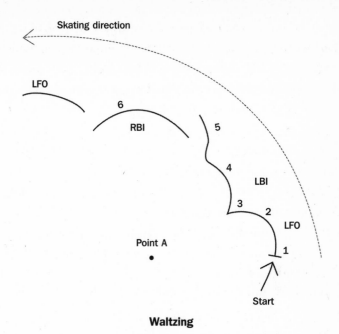

Waltzing

- As you transfer your weight, extend your free left foot in front, down and over your tracing.
- Rotate your head to the outside of your circle to prepare for the last move, the left forward outside edge.
- Do a backward Back outside mohawk from right back outside to left forward outside.
- While on your right back outside edge, keep your head, arms, and shoulders rotating to the outside of your circle as you bring the heel of your left foot to the instep of your right.
- At this point, your upper body is turned to the outside of your circle. (6)
- Bring your free left foot into the instep of your skating foot with the toe turned out at least ninety degrees and bend

both knees. You are now in position to transfer your weight to your left forward outside edge. This completes the waltz step with a RBO-LFO Mohawk.

- As you exit your back Mohawk on your left outside edge, hold your free right foot behind your tracing.
- Hold this edge until you feel it start to slow down. Then stop. This completes the three moves that make up waltzing.
- Practice your waltzing on the other foot.
- When you have learned to do both sides, you can combine them and do alternating waltz steps.
- To combine the two sides: Hold the last edge (which would be an FO edge), bring your free foot in to your skating foot as you transfer your lean to your other foot, and start waltzing in the opposite direction.

You can also repeat your waltzing step in a circle in the same direction: when you complete your waltzing and are on the last step, an FO edge:

- Swing the free foot forward then glide on two feet. While on the same circle, place your weight to your FO edge and continue waltzing.

Are you ready to spin?

In order to spin, you should make sure your forward-outside-to-back-inside three turn has excellent control and speed.

SPINS

Many things in figure skating depend on preparation, but spins are more dependent on preparation than any other move. Most people have a natural sense of spinning direction that is counterclockwise. The instructions here for spinning and jumping are for those skaters.

Two-foot spin: counterclockwise

Start

The Two-Foot Spin

For your first spin, you are going to enter the spin on two feet and shift your weight to create the spinning motion.

- Start in a "T" position with your left heel at your left instep. Keep your arms out to your sides and your eyes looking ahead in the direction you are skating. (1)

- Take two strokes, one on your left foot and one on your right.

- Glide on two feet with your weight evenly divided on two bent knees. Your feet will be about twelve inches apart. (2)

- Now, shift most of your weight to your right side. Both knees will be bent, but the right knee should be bent more deeply. Rotate your arms and shoulders to your right. Make sure your left arm is across your body and your left shoulder is forward; your right arm and shoulder will be back. Let your feet separate to about twenty-four inches apart. (3)

Now, the last shift of weight:

- While keeping your left arm across your body and your left shoulder forward, and the right arm and shoulder back, shift your weight to your left side by swinging your upper body to your left.

- Both knees are bent, but the left knee should be bent more deeply so that you will feel most of your weight over your left outside edge. (4) You will be making a coil tracing.
- Keep this position, with your upper body pressed to your left with a straight back, as your tracing coils to your left.
- Come up in both knees so that you are equally balanced on two feet, which are now about six inches apart. (5)
- Your arms will move out to your sides, with your fingertips at waist level.

The preparation is done, and you are now spinning on the balls of your two feet. Keep your feet parallel to each other and think of pulling them together. The force of your spin will create a tendency for your feet to pull apart. If that happens the spin will slow down—just what you don't want.

- Bring your arms in across your chest toward the end of the spin, when your speed starts to slow down. If you do this arm movement at the right time, you will feel an increase in the speed of your spin. The final arm position is with your elbows at your sides, your wrists crossed, your hands under your chin and flat on your upper chest.
- Finish your spin by exiting on a right back outside edge. Hold for six counts.
- Look over your left shoulder and do a Backward outside mohawk to a left forward outside edge.

You're beginning to combine the moves you've learned into patterns—the real art of skating.

The most common mistake in learning to spin is in the shape of your coil, which is the preparation of your spin. The coil must decrease in size, it must be close to one full circle, and the distance between the beginning of the coil and the spin starting should be no farther away from the start of your coil than your height distance.

> **Tip:** One-foot spins should make tracings that are round circles, not loops, and the round circles should be on top of one another. When skaters do a spin where the tracings are loops that start in one place and end in another, we call this traveling. "Your spin traveled." You don't want to travel. An incomplete coil, or too large a coil tracing on your LFO edge before your spin, is the usual cause of traveling.

If your coil isn't decreasing in size you won't be able to build up the power for your spin. Make sure you are deeply bent in your skating ankles and knees.

The One-Foot Spin

The one-foot spin is identical to the two-foot spin up to step (4). At this point, as you shift your weight, you will also pick up your right foot, so that you are balancing and spinning solely on your left foot. The instep of your right foot should touch the inside of your left knee. As in the two-foot spin, you will bring your arms into your body toward the end of the spin to increase your speed. Always exit with your head up.

A good spin for the beginner is about six revolutions. Your tracing on the ice is what you will look at to count your revolutions.

Once you master the preparation, the spin is not that difficult. Simply stand up straight, relax your body, and feel when your speed starts to decrease so you know when to bring in your arms and when to exit the spin. Spinning is actually very relaxing, but getting the preparation correct before the spin takes a lot of practice and close attention to how your body feels.

Of course, saying "stand up straight" and actually doing it are two very different things. Tension can make the body tight and distort your posture. If you do three spins in a row that get progressively worse, make yourself stop. Practice something else.

Then come back to the spin with a new frame of mind and your body more relaxed. (The same advice does *not* apply to other moves in skating. If you are doing another move, and it gets progressively worse, analyze your tracings, go over each position, make sure your speed and positions are appropriate for the move, and do it again.)

You've learned the basic spin, the one-foot spin. This is just the beginning. Here are some of the conventional position spins: the scratch spin, the sits, the camel, the layback, and the broken leg spin.

Why do they have funny names? In the scratch spin you don't scratch yourself. It's called a scratch spin because the first toe pick scratches the ice surface ever so slightly. In the sits spin you don't sit on the ice, but you are in a low position to the ice with one knee deeply bent and the other leg extended in front of you. The camel spin is a spin in the arabesque position, with the body bent at the hip, the free leg extended back, and the arms at the side. When it's done wrong, it looks like a camel with a hump—but when it's done right, it is beautiful. The layback spin is the only one whose name makes sense. In this position the skater is leaning back while spinning on one foot. In the broken leg spin, one leg only looks broken; you don't break your leg doing it. It is a spin done with the free leg out to the side and bent at the knee.

In 2003, Lucinda Ruh from Switzerland successfully broke the Guinness World Record for the longest continuous spin on one foot. It was 115 revolutions! Besides the length of her spins, her relaxed body position was impressive during the spin. She was as straight as a pin and just held it, and held it, and held it.

> **Tip:** In learning spins and jumps, you will learn the value of using opposite forces. If you want to spin to the left, you'll prepare by winding up in the opposite direction, to the right. If you want to jump up, you'll press in the opposite direction—down—before you jump up. To strengthen your skating, practice the one-foot spin on the right foot as well as the left foot.

ARE YOU RIGHT-FOOTED OR LEFT-FOOTED?

By the time you finish kindergarten, you know if you are right- or left-handed. But how do you know if you are right- or left-footed? Most people are right-handed and left-footed. These instructions have been for the left-footed skater. Do you think you are a left-footed skater?

The following exercise will help you to answer this question. Go to the railing of the rink. Have your back toward the railing and hold onto it with both hands. You'll be facing the center of the rink.

Now imagine a soccer ball coming straight at you. Think fast: Which foot would you stand on?

Most people would balance on their left foot and kick with their right foot. This indicates that they are left-footed, and therefore they will do jumps and spins in a counterclockwise direction, left to right.

For every rule, there are exceptions. You may be the exception, and if you are, that is all right. Just make sure that you jump and spin in the *same* direction. You can't have your jumps counterclockwise and your spins clockwise. Otherwise, when you get to double and multi-revolution jumps, you will have to go back and re-learn one direction so that both your jumps and spins go in the same direction.

Statistics tell us that one out of every ten people is left-handed. There are no statistics on how many skaters are right-footed (meaning they jump and spin clockwise, to the right).

Your skating will be more interesting if you practice both your strong and weak directions in the basic jumps and spins. Some skaters are ambidextrous.

Tip: Most rinks encourage skaters to skate in a counter-clockwise direction. If you are one of the few skaters who naturally rotate the opposite way, a right-footed skater, plan to be the most polite skater on the ice as you say, "Excuse me" and "I'm sorry" to the many skaters going in the other, more common direction.

CHAPTER SIX

FEELING LIKE A STAR

Now you have enough moves to make up a program! You have probably watched the experts skating their programs on television. Did you know that every move they make is planned about a year in advance? Their entire program is designed to match the music and to tell a story. Their makeup and costumes are also carefully planned to get the best effect.

You don't see local skating competitions on television. At the lower levels, skaters who know the skills and techniques described in this book compete by skating a program that is judged against other skaters of the same age and ability level. This chapter will teach you some more moves to include in a program of your own. They look great and are fun to do. Of course, you can feel like a skating star without a program. You may want to do these moves just for the pleasure of doing them. That's fine, too.

If you've studied gymnastics, you will find some of these skating moves quite easy to learn. Top skaters often supplement their training with gymnastics, ballet, fencing, yoga, and tai chi. Using one sport to help you learn another is called cross-training. If you are interested in cross-training, you can discuss the options with your skating instructor. Choose an activity you enjoy to begin with; then, if your instructor agrees that it will help your progress, go for it!

Choosing Music for a Program

The first step in creating a program is to pick out your music. Take your time, and choose something you really like, because you will be hearing it over and over again. For a novice skater who wants to make up a program just for fun, with no intention of testing or competition, the music should last about a minute and a half. Compare this with Olympic programs, which last up to four-and-a-half minutes! The simplest, no-frills way of finding a musical selection is to use the beginning of a musical piece and fade out after one-and-a-half minutes. This approach gives you a well-defined beginning and an acceptable ending.

If you plan to use this music for a test or competition it must last a specific amount of time, according to the rules of the test or competition. Both tests and competitions allow a ten-second leeway over the specific time. The length can also be shorter than the specified time. Within the time frame, your music should have a change of pace. Overtures to Broadway shows are good for this reason—many of them change tempo from fast to slow or slow to fast. Some skaters get a recording studio to combine several parts of one piece of music. Some multi-talented skaters can even do this themselves. Ask the staff at your rink if they prefer cassette tapes or CDs. Most rinks have one or more people who can do the job of cutting music for you.

Your musical selection can be vocal, but instrumental music is a better choice. Most indoor rinks do not have the acoustics that make vocals sound good. Over the years, skaters have used certain popular pieces of music over and over again. A good example is the overture to *The Sound of Music* from the film. Skaters often use the first sixty seconds, cut out the next 3:50 (three minutes, fifty seconds), and use the last thirty-five seconds. Total time: 1:35.

PUTTING A PROGRAM TOGETHER

Whether you are a beginner or an Olympic skater, these guidelines can help you put a program together.

Once you have chosen your music, the next step is to work out a plan. There are two ways of doing this. Either way, you are going to start by making a list of the skating moves you want to include. If you are making up your program for a test or competition, you have little choice as to your moves—you will do the moves that are required by the test or competition. Check the rulebook. Most rinks are members of the ISI (Ice Skating Institute) and/or the USFSA (United States Figure Skating Association). It is a common practice for skaters to start with the ISI tests, and then go to the USFSA testing schedule.

In both associations, you must read the rulebook carefully. Make sure your copy is up to date, because the rules are always being changed and refined. You will lose points from your score if you don't include all the required moves, or if you put in moves that are not allowed at your level. Sometimes there is a choice between two different moves.

If you are making up a program just for fun, it is simpler: just make a list of the moves you enjoy doing. But don't be afraid to add a couple of moves that you haven't yet mastered. Working on a program is an excellent way to motivate yourself to learn something new.

Think about your program in terms of three equal sections. After making your list of moves, listen to the first third of your music. During this part of your program, you should cover the ice and reach out to the audience. Performing in a skating rink is like performing in a theater in the round. The audience is all around you. Back crossovers are a way of covering the ice quickly, yet facing as much of your audience as possible. For this reason, it is common to open a program with back crossovers in both directions. Also, in your first third you should include a move that you are particularly comfortable with—one that looks impressive yet feels secure.

In the second third of your program you want to accomplish two things: do the required moves that don't fit the music elsewhere, and use the slower tempo to catch your breath (you will need it in the last third of your program). This is the time for combination jumps, required footwork, and other required moves that are not appropriate in the other two parts of your music.

The last third of your program shows how well a skater has prepared. This is where endurance is important. The last third has to include any required move that you haven't yet done, as well as any required move that is planned for this last part of your music. You also want to leave the audience with something memorable. Sasha Cohen developed her outstanding forward arabesque done at top speed for this part of her program. Choose a move that is daring and different from those used by other skaters. It also has to be a move with which you feel very secure. It should say something about you, and about how you feel about skating. When you watch professional skaters complete their program, you'll understand why their final moves are so important.

Many programs end with a spin. There are several reasons for this. Often, the music reaches a level of drama that seems to call for a spin. In addition, after a spin, most skaters are a little dizzy, so that is not a good time to do a challenging move. When the spin is at the end, you don't have to worry about recovering from it. You just stop, hold the position, catch your bearings, and bow. It's important to hold your last position of the program—the one just before your bow. It encourages appreciation from the audience. Plan to hold that last stop for six seconds. After that, it is traditional to do two bows.

Tip: Here's a trick that makes you and the audience feel good when you take your two bows. On the first bow, you say to yourself, "Thanks for watching me," and on the second bow, you say to yourself, "I loved skating for you!"

The first time you do your program with the ice cleared of other skaters can be scary and exciting at the same time.

Planning a program is a good goal, even if your repertoire includes only a few very basic moves. For example, here is a program for a skater who has only learned forward skating, forward crossovers, turning, a snowplow stop and an attempt at a two-foot spin. The music is the first minute and a half from the overture to the film version of *Chicago*. If you feel this program is not challenging you, substitute more advanced moves, and use your upper body and arms to bring out the music.

- Start in the middle of the ice with your right heel in the ice.

- After the first phrase of music, which is twenty seconds long, bring your feet together and start your program.

- Take three short strokes (left, right, left), and glide on two feet. Repeat one more time, ending with a snowplow stop. (1)

- Do three forward crossovers in the counterclockwise direction (right foot over left), ending with a snowplow stop. Turn. (2)

- Do three forward crossovers in a clockwise direction (left foot over right), ending with a snowplow stop. (3)

- Take two strong strokes, then glide on two feet with your arms out. Repeat once again. (4)

- Aiming at the centerline of the rink, take two forward strokes. (5)

> **Tip:** If you watch skaters on television, you'll notice that their starting position is usually a dramatic pose, often with one toe in the ice. That's great for a skater who is advanced, but for a novice, putting the heel in the ice is easier and more secure. Use the heel in the ice position until you reach a higher level of balance and coordination.

- Glide on two feet, then slow down by using a snowplow stop as you wind up your arms to do a two-foot spin. (6)

- At the end of the spin, put the heel of your right blade in the ice and your arms out. Hold this for three seconds. (7)

- Bring your feet together. Hold this position for six seconds. Take your two bows, smile at the crowd, and exit the ice.

That's it—your first program.

In any program, you must memorize the elements and the skating direction. Picture the tracings you want to make on the ice. Drawing the skating program on paper can help. It may look like a confusing scribble at first, but as you mentally review the moves, it will begin to make sense for you.

Opposite is a sketch of the *Chicago* program described above. You should be able to understand the skating choreography. Can you?

FORWARD ARABESQUE

Variations of the arabesque are taught in ballet and gymnastics as well as skating. In skating you must be able to balance solidly on one foot, lean forward from your hips, arch your back, stretch your free leg and both arms, and tilt the head up.

There are many different arabesques in skating. The first one to learn is the forward arabesque, done in a straight line, on both edges of the blade. This is called "doing the arabesque on the flat."

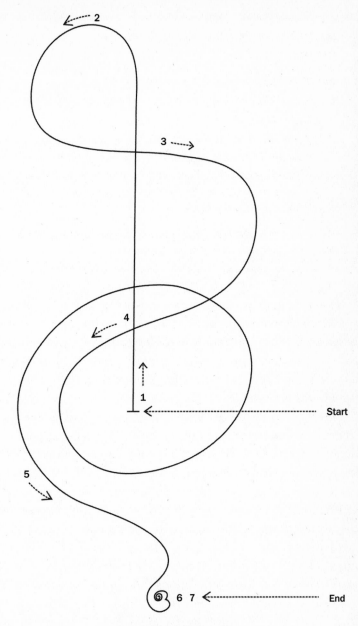

Start

End

Chicago **choreography**

Are you ready to do a forward arabesque?

You have to be able to do two things well:

1. Balance on one foot while skating in a straight line for six or more beats.

2. Lean forward at your waist, lift the foot of your free leg higher than your hip and, at the same time, arch the top of your body. This arch means that your head is higher than your skating hip. Your arms will be out to the sides for balance.

As you improve your arabesque, you will also work on the arch between your shoulder blades.

The term arabesque is borrowed from ballet. The position is slightly different in figure skating, in that the upper body is lower than what is generally considered the proper position in ballet. Also, ballerinas generally perform their arabesques with one arm extended in front, while skaters do it with many different arm positions.

Skaters tend to use the term spirals, rather than arabesques. There is an interesting reason for this. Originally, a spiral was done on a very bent knee. As you know by now, a deeply bent knee makes a circle that decreases in its size. The tracing of the early skaters' arabesque was a coil, or spiral shape, so it made sense to call it a spiral. Today, when the arabesque is mastered, the skating knee is not bent. If the arabesque is done on an edge, the tracing is a large curve. If it is done on a flat, the tracing is a long straight line. It no longer resembles a spiral shape at all. The two skating associations don't agree on a name. The ISI calls it an arabesque, and the USFSA, which was founded long before the ISI, still calls it a spiral. I call it an arabesque.

It's a good idea to spend some time working on the

> **Tip:** To test whether your arms are in the right position, imagine a line going from the fingernail on your left pointer finger through your left ear lobe, out your right ear lobe and touching the fingernail on your right pointer finger. Think of this imaginary line, which is parallel to the floor (or ice, when you're at the rink), as you do the arabesque.

arabesque position at home, in front of a mirror, before trying it on the ice. If you are a gymnast or a ballet student, you have probably practiced the move already. If the arabesque is new to you, start by feeling the position while standing on two feet.

Here's how to do it:

- Facing a mirror, stand with your feet parallel and about six inches apart.
- Reach your arms up above your head.
- As you bring your arms down, pull your hips back, so that they are slightly behind your knees, and your knees are slightly behind your ankles.
- With your arms stretched out to your sides, stretch the top of your body forward. Your goal is to get the top of your body parallel to the floor with your head up, eyes looking into the mirror ahead of you.

When you are ready to do the arabesque position on one foot, you will need something to help your balance. A chair will do.

- Put the chair between you and the mirror, with the seat facing you.
- With your hands resting on the seat of the chair, move your feet as far back as possible so that you are still holding onto the chair, but the top of your body is stretched forward over the seat.

- Lift your right leg behind you while keeping your head up, so that you see your reflection in the mirror.
- Keep your right knee straight and allow your upper body to go down, toward the chair.
- Make sure your weight is solidly over your left foot. Remember to keep your head up. Your goal, over the next few weeks or months, is to be able to see your foot over your head when you look in the mirror.

Are you ready to take your arabesque from the floor to the ice?

If you can balance for six beats on your left foot when you practice the arabesque position on the floor at home, and have at least a ninety degree angle between your two legs, you are ready to put it together on the ice.

Even if you are limber enough to raise your free foot higher than your head when you practice the arabesque position on the floor, your foot will not be that high when you do it on the ice. Part of the reason is the fact that the heel of your skate is about two inches high. Those two inches make a big difference in your balance and security. In addition, the weight of your skate makes it harder to lift your leg.

When you practice the arabesque at home in front of a mirror, your main objective is to stretch your free leg muscles against your skating leg muscles. When you do it on the ice, your objective is different: it is to balance in a straight line with your head up and your arms out to your sides. The height of your free leg is less important at this stage.

Here's what to do when you work on the arabesque while skating:

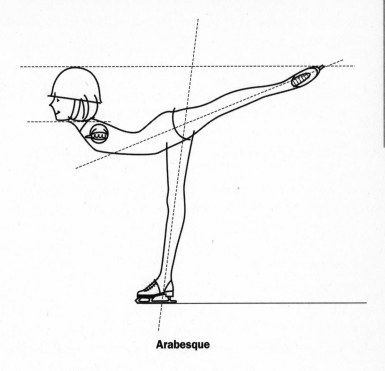

Arabesque

- Start at one end of the rink and take a couple of long strokes to build speed.

- Glide on two feet for a short time as you straighten your posture in preparation for your forward arabesque on a left flat.

- Keep your head up and look straight ahead. If you can choose something to look at, this will help. Many rinks have posters of their sponsors on their railings. Choose something that doesn't move, because you will be using the line from you to your reference point to follow as your straight axis.

- Slowly bring your right foot about six inches in front of you and close to the ice.

> **Tip:** Often in ice skating, you have to feel what you are doing without looking. In an arabesque, you can't look at where you've placed your free foot. If you did, your change of position would throw you off balance. Learn the feel of the position off the ice, then remember that feeling as you skate the move.

- As you bring the right foot back behind you, allow your upper body to lean forward with your arms extended to your sides. In the beginning you don't have to get the free leg very high; your object is to maintain a straight line on your left blade.

While skating on the left foot in a straight line, stretch your right leg (your free leg) right behind your right hip. Don't let it go to either side. Having your right foot go forward, then behind you, will help, but it does not guarantee that the foot will be directly behind your hip. It takes practice to get the feel for this position.

As your free leg goes back, and your upper body goes forward, you will feel like a seesaw. If the free foot goes up too quickly, or the top of the body goes down too quickly, you will be off balance. The arabesque is a vulnerable position in many ways. That is why it is important to take your time in learning the happy medium of balance in this move. If you hold the attempted arabesque for only a few seconds and then balance on two feet and try again, you will learn the feeling of balance.

While you are learning to do the arabesque, you can keep your skating knee slightly bent. Sure, it looks better with the skating knee absolutely straight and confident looking, but safety is more important. If a novice skater hits a rut in the ice, she is going to fall forward over her left toe pick. Because her arms are out and her hands are stretched away from her body, she will not have the time nor the coordination to use her arms to protect herself. The result is a nasty, mean fall.

Keep the skating knee slightly bent when working on your arabesque for the first year of practice. With the knee slightly bent, you are able to catch a fall by bending deeper, and either sliding into a forward fall on one side, or maybe recovering your balance and not falling at all.

Arabesques are beautiful skating moves. You will feel like a bird in flight when you master them. You'll feel the arch between your head and your free foot, as well as the arch between your shoulder blades that stretches to the tips of your fingers. The arabesque is worth working on!

Are you ready to do the lunge?

Before you try it, you should be able to balance for at least six beats on your right foot, and be limber in the lunge position. Unlike the arabesque, this move can only be practiced at the rink because it requires the slipperiness of the ice. Start by practicing the position while you hold onto the railing. Remember to watch for other skaters before you try it.

FORWARD LUNGE

This move is sometimes called a drag, because you are dragging one leg behind the other. Lunge makes sense, too. It is a dance term.

Here's how to understand and feel the position of the lunge:

- Stand about twelve inches away from the railing. Place your right heel at your left instep in a "T" position. Stretch out both arms and put your hands on the railing to steady yourself.

- Turn your upper body to your right, in the direction that you'll be going.

- Let your right foot slide slightly forward. Keep most of your weight over this right foot. Your right ankle and knee will start to bend.

- Keep your left ankle and knee straight, with the left blade still facing the railing.

- Let the right foot continue to slide away from the left.

- Keep both hands on the railing (so you don't excessively stretch the muscles on the inside of your left leg).

- When you start to feel a pull, come back to your original "T" position. Your goal is to get in a full lunge position, with your upper body perpendicular to the ice, your right ankle and knee fully bent, and your left leg stretched out so that the knee of your left leg is lower than your right knee. The boot, not the blade, of the left foot will be on the ice.

It will take time to stretch your muscles for the lunge. Don't be surprised if it takes weeks, or months.

The forward lunge is a beautiful position to do and to watch. It is also very helpful in stretching your muscles so you can turn out your legs in relation to your hips. When you first try the lunge, don't focus too much on your body position. It's more important to concentrate on your balance and the tracing you make on the ice. You should do the lunge in a straight line, on the flat of your blade.

Tip: Practice the lunge on both sides. You will be stretching and strengthening your adductors, the inside leg muscles that hold up your free leg when you are skating. The stronger these muscles are, the stronger your skating will be.

Here's an exercise for practicing the lunge:

- Start in your "T" position. Take two strokes to get a bit of speed.

- Place your free foot beside your skating foot as you balance on two feet while choosing a point to look at for your imaginary axis.

- Balance on your right foot while placing the left foot behind and turned out ninety degrees.

- Think about feeling the position, not looking at it. If you try to look at your free foot, you won't be able to skate in a straight line, and if you are not on a straight line, you're not going to be able to place your free foot behind you. Look straight ahead and feel your left foot turning out ninety degrees.

- With both your arms extended to your sides, and your eyes looking straight ahead, bend your right ankle and knee. If your left foot is turned out enough, and placed properly behind, the inside edge of the blade of the left foot will drag on the ice.

- As you gradually bend deeper, the leather part of the left boot will eventually drag on the ice for your final bending position in the lunge.

While mastering the lunge you have to use another skating sense: your hearing. When your left blade is dragging on the ice, you will hear the sound of it scraping. When you bend deeper in your right ankle and knee, the left blade will clear the ice by about one inch, and the leather part of the boot will touch the surface. There will be no sound. Assuming that your back is straight and your shoulders are square over your hips, when you get to this point of hearing no sound from your left skate, you will know you are in the correct position. Advanced skaters like this "silent lunge" position because when the leather

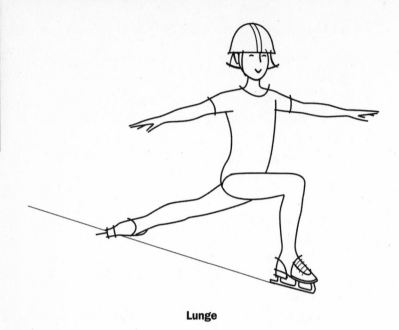

Lunge

part of the boot—not the blade—is dragging on the ice, there is very little resistance, so they are able to maintain their speed. Make sure your arms are extended proudly and your head is up, with your chin lifted slightly. This is a confident position.

Sorry, you're not done yet! This move doesn't end with some-one helping you up from your lunge! The next part takes pure muscle strength.

- From the lunge position, come up on one foot, with your free foot held behind and your arms extended. To build your strength for this, practice holding the lunge for a short time, increasing the time gradually. The longer you hold it, the more difficult it is to get up.

- To get up, let the top of your body go forward slightly— about four inches. With your arms extended, pull your shoulder blades together as you engage your thigh muscles of your right leg and straighten out your very bent right knee to a straight position.

- In your final position you will have your head up, your arms extended to your sides, back straight, skating knee straight but not locked, and your free leg off the ice and extended behind you and held high.

The beauty of doing the lunge is the contrast between the positions during the lunge and after it. Don't be surprised, when you first work on coming up into the final position, if you hear yourself give a grunt or a groan. It happens more often than not.

Go slowly. If you are not yet physically strong enough to do the lunge and return to an upright position, strengthen your muscles by doing flexibility exercises. Here's a good one.

Deep Bending on One Foot

Work on both your left and your right thigh muscles, because you'll be doing the lunge on both sides. Let's start with the right side.

- Stand on your right foot, holding on to a railing if you are at the rink, or a heavy chair if you are doing your exercises at home.

- Tuck your left foot behind your right knee.

- Bend, being careful to keep your back straight.

- When you reach the point where you're squeezing your left foot, gradually return to the standing position.

- Do this move with steady timing; six beats as you bend down, and six beats as you return to your starting position. Make yourself count evenly. Repeat once on the other foot.

In the beginning, do this exercise only once on each side. The next day, do it twice. Work up to doing it six times in succession. Decide on increasing your repetitions according to the way your muscles feel. Listen to your body.

Working on the lunge on both the right and the left foot will help you with other moves in skating. It teaches you to keep a straight back while doing deep bending and turning one hip, knee, and ankle against the other leg. Some skaters use the lunge as part of their warm-up.

SHOOT-THE-DUCK

Here's another skating move with a funny name: the shoot-the-duck.

The shoot-the-duck uses your back muscles in a completely different way than they were used on your arabesque (arched), or your lunge (pulled up and back). Your back muscles will be drawn forward, in, and together.

The warm up for the shoot-the-duck is the "touch your toes" exercise. Do this with your knees slightly bent, so that when you come out of the position, you don't put undue strain on your lower back muscles. If you are doing this with your two-inch-high-heeled ice skates on, bend both knees even more than when you practice at home in no shoes, or flat shoes.

> **Tip:** Some people who have limber bodies are disappointed when they can't touch their toes in this very basic exercise. If you find this is true, do not be concerned. The reason may have to do with your bodily proportions—the length of your arms in relation to the length of your legs. You can still learn to do the shoot-the-duck.

Here's how to do the touch-your-toes exercise off the ice:

- Stand with your back straight and your feet parallel.

- Reach up with both arms, until you feel a big stretch in your back.

- With your knees slightly bent, and your head looking straight ahead, not down, slowly start to reach for your toes.

- Keep your head up, so that your eyes are looking straight ahead.

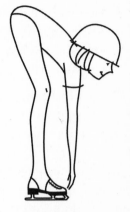

Exercise for shoot-the-duck

- Feel the muscles under your chin squeeze. This is very close to the position that you will be in, when you try the shoot-the-duck on the ice.

- Return to your starting position slowly, keeping your head up all the time.

When you are ready to try the shoot-the-duck on the ice, first do it with your balance on your left foot. Later, as with the arabesque, and the lunge, you will do the shoot-the-duck on both the right and the left foot.

Since you will be practicing on your left foot first, you'll need to have enough strength in your left thigh to come back up after the shoot-the-duck position. To strengthen your thigh muscles, practice the same exercise that you did for the exit from your lunge. To remind you:

- Stand on one foot, holding onto something for balance.

- With one foot tucked in behind the knee of the other foot, bend to a count of six.

- Make sure that you don't pop up in your knee when you come up.
- Use six beats to bend down and six beats to come up. Keep your head looking straight ahead throughout this exercise. Do it on the other foot for body strengthening. Go cautiously—listen to your body.

Do you feel ready to try the shoot-the-duck on the ice? Like the arabesque and the lunge, the important thing in the beginning is getting the pattern correct. The position of your body will come later.

Use the same preparation as you used with the arabesque and the lunge: Take two strokes forward for speed, then bring your free foot into your skating foot as you glide on two feet while lining up your body by focusing on a point straight ahead. Transfer your weight to your left flat; bring both arms forward as your upper body leans over your left knee. Your arms will be forward and pressed toward the ice. Bend your left knee deeply. Keep your head up, eyes straight ahead.

Tip: How to avoid falling backward during a shoot-the-duck.

1. Keep your free leg low. Don't put your hands under your free leg. It will cause the free leg to lift up. If you do, it changes your balance from "good and secure" to "beyond the point of return." It will cause your back to be erect instead of pressing forward.

2. Usually you want your back to be erect (perpendicular to the ice), but in shoot-the-duck, an erect back will cause your center of balance to go back over the last third of your blade, and down you go. Keep your back straight, but lean forward from your hips.

Shoot-the-duck

You'll need to coordinate the timing of the two key parts of this move—leaning the top of your body forward and bending your skating knee. If you lean forward too quickly, your weight will be too far forward. On the other hand, if you bend your skating knee too quickly, your balance will go backwards, off the heel of your skating foot.

It will take time and patience to coordinate these two motions. You will take some spills. But don't worry, they aren't the type of spills that hurt, because you are already low to the ice. You will slide, not stumble.

The shoot-the-duck is one of the few positions in figure skating in which you want your shoulders to be ahead of your hips. Usually, you are working to get your shoulders over your hips.

Look at the illustration carefully to see the position for which you are aiming. Keep your head up, with your eyes straight ahead, your arms forward and relaxed, and your hands resting lightly on your free leg. Press your chest toward your skating knee. The skating leg is so bent that it feels pressed down. The angle of the back is almost parallel to the angle of the skating leg, from the knee to the ankle.

Are you ready to learn the waltz jump?

Before learning the waltz jump, make sure your forward outside and back outside edges are controlled and you feel confident.

THE WALTZ JUMP

The waltz jump is the first jump that most skaters learn. Assuming you are a left-footed skater, the basic idea is to skate forward on your left foot, jump lightly off your left toe pick, kick the right leg as you rotate the body while in the air, and land on the right toe pick, skating backward. In other words, it is a frontward-to-backward move.

Here's how to do the waltz jump:

- Start in a "T" position with your left heel at your right instep.
- As you bend deeply to push onto your left forward outside edge, allow both your arms to go back so that your shoulder blades are pinched. (1)
- Glide on your left forward outside edge.
- Extend your free right leg back over your tracing.
- Bend your left knee for the liftoff into your left toe pick.
- Swing your free right foot forward, allowing your right knee to straighten so that the leg moves like a pendulum with force.
- Bring your right arm forward and up to assist in getting height to your jump.
- Both arms will be out to your sides. (2)
- As you land press your left arm forward. (3)

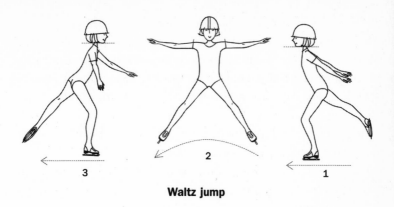

Waltz jump

Your body will leave the ice as your free foot passes your skating foot. Your bottom toe pick will penetrate the ice both on the takeoff and on the landing. In the air, your goal will be to have both knees straight, your torso erect, and your head held high. Now both arms will be out to your sides. When you land on your right back outside edge, bend deeply in your knee to soften the impact and to feel the grace of this jump. As you

Tip: Check your tracings.

When you analyze your tracing after a waltz jump, you may find a scrape mark on the takeoff. This means your takeoff foot was turning on the ice before you lifted off— a mistake that is sometimes called "skating sideward." To correct this error, make sure your blades are sharp enough, and make sure you're bending enough just before lifting off.

The landing tracing should look like a mirror image of the takeoff edge. If it doesn't—if it has a little half-three turn—you are not doing a full 180-degree rotation in the air.

land, your left arm and shoulder should be forward, and your right arm and shoulder should be to your right side for a checked position. Midway through the exit edge, slowly come up in your right knee and move the left arm from in front to your left side. Your right arm remains to your right side. At the end of your exit edge, turn your head to your left. Do a backward outside Mohawk onto your left forward outside edge. Practice this basic jump in both directions

Congratulations! You've done your first jump. Practice it in both directions and as often as you can—and get ready to move up to the next level.

CHAPTER SEVEN

FUN WITH A PARTNER

Today, a figure skating team can be made up of a man and a woman, but it wasn't always that way. Until the last part of the nineteenth century, it was a team of two men or two women. Then, in 1888 in Vienna, Austria, a "mixed pair" joined the pair competition. Of course, Vienna was a natural for this, since it was already home to the romantic Strauss waltz done by a man and a woman. In the years that followed, mixed pairs became the acceptable style. Recently, having two men or two women compete in pairs has been re-introduced and accepted.

The first (and perhaps biggest) challenge of pair skating is finding a partner. The ratio of men to women in figure skating is about 1:9. That's great if you're a guy, but not so easy if you're a girl.

Skaters don't usually just start skating with a partner. A partnership usually evolves when two skaters occasionally practice skating moves together, then become serious about doing it on a regular basis. Before long, they hear that other people enjoy seeing them skate together. After many practice sessions, perhaps over years, they are ready for testing and competitions.

There are two kinds of partnering: pair skating and ice dancing. Pair skating takes two strong and gutsy free-style skaters. The very names of some of the required moves will give you an idea of the challenges that pair skaters face: the death spiral, the throw axel, and the platter lift. In the platter lift the male skater lifts his partner above his head. Her body is stretched out like a dinner platter. Most skaters agree that pair skating is more dangerous than solo freestyle skating or ice dancing.

Ice dancing requires two skaters with strong edges, footwork, music interpretation, and the skill of carefully reading the rulebook of allowed moves. The rules of ice dancing for tests and competitions are very specific. They do not permit throws, the lifting of a partner higher than the lifter's shoulders, or most spins. These rules limit ice dancers to very fine footwork and musical interpretation—which must be done quickly and (to the audience) effortlessly. Ice dancers also face more restrictions on their choice of music.

Both pair skating and ice dancing require an enormous amount of training to get to a national level. Pair skaters work on their timing for their acrobatic lifts, jumps, throws, and innovative spins. Ice dancers work endlessly on fine, tiny steps and imaginative hand and arm positions. Many solo skaters also compete in pair skating, but rarely in ice dancing. Pair skaters almost never compete in ice dancing at a national level. That's because the requirements of ice dancing are so restrictive.

Those who skate with a partner think it is both more fun and more challenging to skate together without mistakes. It's easy to get out of unison, and a mistake is obvious when one member of a pair team slips or forgets what move comes next. Those who prefer to skate alone love it because they don't have to deal with the challenges of having a partner. They simply enjoy skating by themselves.

Two different body types often determine whether skaters become ice dancers or pair skaters. If you've watched figure-skating competitions on television, you might guess what they are. Generally speaking, both male and female ice dancers are tall with lean legs. In pair skating, the guy is often twelve inches taller than his partner. He is big, strong in body and in skating ability. She is tiny, but has muscles like steel. Both are gutsy and strong, consistent jumpers.

ICE DANCING

When you begin working with a partner, you will not do anything risky; you won't even do turns. You'll start out doing forward skating together—first, in a "hand to shoulder" position, then in a compulsory dance position. This sounds simple, but you'll be amazed at how difficult it is to stay together.

The Hand-to-Shoulder Position

Talk with your partner and agree on how many beats you are going to hold each stroke. To start, try a pattern of six beats; two beats on your left foot, two beats on your right foot, then glide on two feet for two beats and repeat.

When you do this first exercise, your goal is to match each other's speed, not to race or compete with each other.

- Stand side by side, about two feet apart. Both skaters face forward in the same direction. Start with the girl on her partner's right side; later you can switch sides.

- Each partner places a hand on the partner's nearer shoulder. Keep your arm straight to maintain the distance between you and your partner.

- Skate down the length of the rink one stroke at a time. Then balancing on two feet. The timing is: two beats each stroke, two beats when on two feet.

- When you come to a corner of the rink, simply glide on two feet, or do a few swizzles if you need to increase your speed.

- After you turn the corner of the rink, straighten your shoulder line so that it is perpendicular to your future skating axis in front of you

- Repeat the exercise.

Tip: This is a good time for both partners to review the five points of posture listed in Chapter One, "Your Body: Your Essential Tool." (Basically: head up, back straight, arms out, skating knee well bent, and free leg fully extended.)

Take turns watching and critiquing each other as you skate around the rink. After you get used to skating together, you'll learn to skate as a unit to the music. Take one step at a time. There's plenty of learning and fun ahead for you.

When you feel comfortable skating in a hand-to-shoulder position, you'll be ready to try two other forward ice dance positions. Learn them in a standing position before trying them on the ice.

The Kilian Position

The first dance that skaters do, the Dutch waltz, is done in the kilian position.

- Both skaters face forward.
- The woman is to the right of her partner, with the back of her left shoulder touching the front of his right shoulder.
- Her left arm will be extended in front of her partner.

Tip: In dance positions, both partners can communicate with each other about their speed and rotation by putting pressure on the arm that is extended. Look at the expressions on the faces of ice dancers to see who is trying to lead, or who's trying to correct a position. Of course, perfect dancers have no tension. All ice dancers aim to have perfect positions at a perfect speed, so that their program is seamless and flows to the music. (It doesn't start that way!)

- The man's right arm is across her back. His right hand and her right hand are together, securely on her right hip.

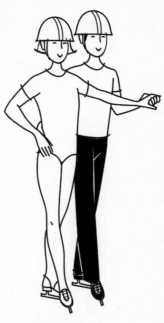

Kilian dance position

Start skating together in the kilian position, using the same six-beat pattern that you used in the hand-to-shoulder position:

- Take two strokes of two beats each. Glide on two feet for two beats. Repeat. Do this down the length of the rink.

- When you come to the corner of the rink, either glide on two feet, or do swizzles until you reach the next corner. Resume skating in the kilian position as you go down the other side of the rink.

The Open Fox-Trot Position

This position, like the kilian position, allows both skaters to face forward.

To get into this position, start by facing your partner as in a waltz hold.

- For the girl: have your partner put his right hand behind you, on your left shoulder blade.

- Put your left arm on top of his right arm.

- Put your left hand on his right shoulder.

- Both partners should keep their elbows up. (The person whose elbow is on the bottom is responsible for this. In this case, it's your partner who will take the blame for any dropped elbows.)

- Your right arm and your partner's left arm will be extended, with your right hand and his left hand clasped.

From the waltz hold you are ready to turn into the open fox-trot position:

- Both partners turn slightly away from one another so that they can skate in the same direction.

- In this open fox-trot position, skate forward in the six-beat pattern.

- The partners will be on their opposite feet. When the guy is skating on his right foot, the girl is on her left.

Open fox-trot position

- As you do the basic six-beat pattern exercise together, try to keep an equal distance between your hips and your partner's hips at all times. This is a firm position, but you can make it look relaxed by having straight backs, keeping your eyes straight ahead, and bending your skating legs and extending your free legs in unison.

The Waltz Position

This dance position has one partner skating forward and one skating backward. As with all your ice dancing moves, practice this one while standing off the ice before trying it on the ice.

The waltz position in ice dancing is similar to ballroom dancing. Here is how it works:

- The partners stand facing each other.
- The girl steps about six inches to her left, so that her right foot is between her partner's two feet. He will make sure that his right foot is also between hers.
- The guy puts his right arm around his partner and places the palm of his hand on her left shoulder blade.
- The girl puts her left fingertips on top of her partner's right shoulder.
- She puts her right hand in her partner's left hand, palms facing each other.
- Each partner looks over the other's right shoulder.

Practice all three of the basic ice dance positions in the basic pair-skating exercise. Everyone can learn the technique, but it's the skater's style and expression that make the difference in high-level ice dancing. Style is something that can't be taught; you either have it or you don't. Coaches and judges recognize it in its early stages.

Waltz position

How to have a secure waltz position

In ice dancing it's important for the partners to feel like a single unit. They both must have firm positions. Neither one has a relaxed or limp arm. The correct posture of each skater helps the team keep a square position and move as a single unit.

There are about twenty compulsory ice dances. They include waltzes, fox-trots, cha-chas, rumbas, and tangos. In the free dance part of ice dancing, there are fourteen named steps and seventeen turns. Many competitive ice dancers say it's not learning the dance moves that is difficult; it's learning the rules. That's an exaggeration, but the rules of ice dancing are restrictive. Be sure to study them carefully if you plan to be tested or compete in ice dancing.

PAIR SKATING

If the words "death spiral," "throw axel," "lasso lift," and "split twists" excite you, you are going to love pair skating. If these names scare you, you are probably going to prefer ice dancing or solo skating. Pair skating is the most dangerous of the figure skating disciplines. The USFSA would like to replace the term "throw" and call it "partner-assisted," but most people in skating still refer to partner-assisted jumps as throw jumps.

Unlike ice dancing, where the requirements for the moves and dances are predetermined, pair skating is less restrictive. But just like ice dancing, pair skating requires lots of practice, good partnership, and cooperation. Like ice dancers, pair skaters are always striving for unison.

Skating in unison is done in two basic styles: mirror skating and shadow skating. A pair that are right- and left-footed would love mirror skating. In mirror skating, both skaters are doing the same moves, but in different directions. When two fast and powerful skaters do this they quickly cover the ice, each skater asking for your attention. The result is electrifying.

In shadow skating, both skaters are doing the same moves in the same direction while maintaining equal distance between their bodies. This is where the smallest mistake will show up like a sore thumb, because the audience sees the two skaters as one unit. Shadow skating is most common.

Tip: If you are a typical female pair partner, your male partner is probably about twelve inches taller than you are. The difference in your heights will be great for advanced moves, but it's difficult in the beginning when you are just working on basic stroking and crossovers. When you begin pair skating in the hand-to-shoulder position, if there is a big height difference, your left arm will be reaching upward. That is unavoidable, so don't be concerned about it at this point.

Basic Pair Positions

When you first start pair skating, you will do the same exercises that are described for ice dancing. In a typical pair position the pattern is two equal strokes for two beats each, then gliding on two feet for two beats, and repeating.

When you are ready to try forward skating and forward crossovers, try this:

A basic pair skating position

- Both partners stand side by side, facing the same direction.
- The girl stands to the right of the guy.
- For the girl: Maintain your right arm extended to your right, your left arm to your left in front of your partner.
- For the guy: Hold your left hand in your partner's left hand (bend your left elbow to facilitate this). Put your right hand on the girl's left hip.
- Practice the six-beat pattern in this new basic pair position.
- When you come to the first corner, the girl will increase her speed in order to lead the way on the crossovers.

Pair position

- After the crossovers, your position will revert back to the starting position with both partners evenly side by side as you skate forward in pattern.
- Continue your practice pattern around the rink.

Every time you practice together, work on your unison and matching each other's grip into the ice before each stroke.

Pair Spins

Pair skaters perform two types of spins: solo spins (done side by side) and pair spins. In a solo spin, both members of the pair do two individual spins at the same time, in the same positions,

> Why is it that in pairs only the female is lifted? Actually,
> there is no rule requiring that only the male partner can
> do the lifting. But, in competition, hardly anyone dares to
> do it the other way; they are afraid of being marked
> down by the judges. Generally speaking, judges tend to
> be conservative.

at the same speed, and with the same number of revolutions. This is not easy, but it looks great when it's done right.

Judges give pair spins higher marks when the two spinners are close to one another. (Of course, spinning too close can risk a collision.) Pair skaters work hard on centering their spins. A spin that travels is very disconcerting to the partner. Some solo spins commonly done by pair skaters are sits spins, camels, and variations of the one-foot spin.

In a pair spin, the partners do one spin holding one another. The two skaters don't have to be in the same position. As you can imagine, the positions for the pair spins are quite varied. Each year, it seems, some pair team comes up with a position that has never been done before.

Pinwheels

This is a fun move for two skaters to do.

In the pair skaters' pinwheel, two partners rotate around a common center spot. When you first do it the closer you are to one another in body weight and height, the easier this will be.

- Start facing each other.
- Both partners stretch out their left arms, then hold each other's left hand, as if shaking hands.
- Keeping your back straight, move away from your partner, so that both partners' left arms are straight.

Tip: Precision skaters also do a move called the pinwheel. In it, usually sixteen skaters line up, eight facing one way and eight facing the opposite direction. Each group of eight skaters rotates around a center point. You'll see this often at ice shows. Audiences love it!

- Both skaters balance on the right foot.
- Both skaters push three times with your left blade.

Keep your left elbow straight during these three pushes. A bent elbow will prevent you from doing the move well. Also,

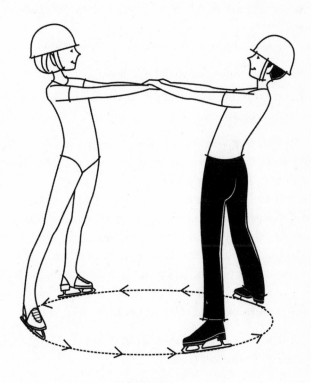

Pinwheel

think of your left hands being over an imaginary spot on the ice. You are both rotating around this spot. The spot does not move; you move around it.

After you have both pushed three times with your left foot, while keeping your left elbow straight,

- Continue to glide in the circle on your RFI edge, as you turn out your left foot, pointing the toe toward the left.
- Place your turned-out left foot on the ice (this puts you in a spread-eagle position).
- Your feet are turned out, with your weight equally distributed. Both feet will be on inside edges. Your left foot will be on an LBI and your right foot will be on an RFI edge. You might say that you are going in two directions at once!

As soon as you are in this spread eagle position,

- Reach for your partner's right hand.
- Keep your elbows straight as you lean back, away from your partner.

If you find that you are not able to keep the handhold when the speed increases, take off your gloves and try doing the pinwheel in bare hands for a better grip.

The last and the most fun thing to do is to increase the speed of the pinwheel by reducing the distance between you and your partner. Do this by bending your elbows, and pretend you are going to touch your partner's nose with your own. If you have already bent your elbows, you won't be able to increase the speed of the pinwheel spin. Keep those elbows straight until you need to bend them to increase your speed at the end of the pinwheel.

- To come out of the pinwheel spin, simply turn to your left then glide on two feet.

What do skaters do when they get dizzy?

You will probably be dizzy when you finish a pinwheel spin. Any time you feel dizzy, you shouldn't skate. To get over the dizzy feeling, look at something that isn't moving, maybe the clock in your rink, then shake your head and look at the object again. This helps you reset your equilibrium. You may have to do it more than once. Everyone is different about feeling dizzy. A move can make you dizzy one day and have no effect the next.

When you are learning the pinwheel spin, you will start by holding left hands, then you and your partner will both spin in a counterclockwise direction (the most common direction for skaters). Practice the pinwheel in the other direction as well. To do that, you will start by holding right hands, with elbows straight, and glide onto your left forward inner edge by pushing with your right blade.

The Wheelbarrow

It's easy to see why this move is called a wheelbarrow. Actually, one skater is the wheelbarrow and the other is the pusher.

- The skater in front will be in the shoot-the-duck position.
- The skater behind will either be in a safe gliding position, or in a beautiful forward arabesque position. For starters, let's work on the safer of the two positions for the skater who is behind.
- Start with the shorter of the two skaters standing in

Wheelbarrow

front of the taller skater. The palms of her hands will be facing the ice.

- The taller skater will stand behind and slightly to the left of the shorter skater. The palms of his hands will be facing up.
- He reaches under his partner's hands so their palms touch each other. This hold is very important to the overall position of the wheelbarrow. His hands are under hers, and both skaters can feel their palms touching.

Now you're ready to move.

- You both should be in the "T" position.
- Take two strokes forward, first on the left and then on the right. Glide on two feet as the skater behind guides his partner so that she is directly in front of him.
- The skater in front starts to go down on two feet, then straightens her right leg in front of her to form the shoot-the-duck position.
- Her arms are back, and held by her partner. Her arms resemble the handles of a wheelbarrow.

The taller skater is in control of their motion. If he feels there is enough speed and the team is going on a straight line, he can go from being safely on two feet to leaning forward on his right foot, with his head held high, as his left leg goes up behind him in an arabesque.

After holding the arabesque position, the taller skater will lower his left leg and glide on two feet. He can lift his hands to help his partner go from the shoot-the-duck to the original standing position, with the taller skater behind and slightly to his partner's left side. As always in the forward arabesque, the taller skater should keep his skating knee slightly bent for safety.

Wheelbarrows are fun to do. Skating clubs often hold fun nights when members perform moves that they never do during practice. Rolling on the ice is one. Having wheelbarrow races is another. Make sure you are pretty proficient before taking chances!

Are you ready for the Dutch Waltz?

You should feel strong and confident in your forward and outside edge swing rolls before learning this dance.

A Dance on Ice: The Dutch Waltz

The Dutch Waltz is the most basic ice dance. It is done in the kilian position, with all steps for both partners being forward. It's enjoyable to do because it's nice to skate to waltz music, and it fits a standard ice rink—one hundred feet by two hundred feet. Like all ice dances, the Dutch Waltz is done to music that meets specific tempo requirements. Skaters become accustomed to the standard musical arrangements that many rinks use.

You have already learned the kilian position; now you're ready to put three new and useful steps together. One of them,

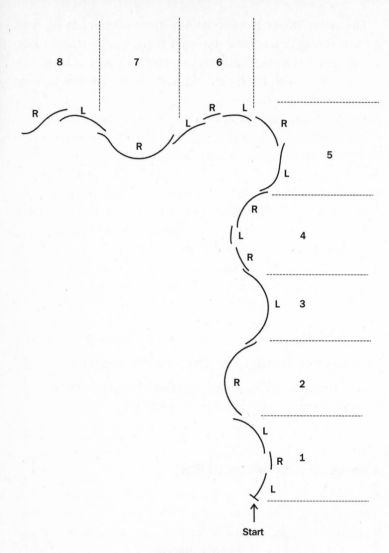

The Dutch Waltz

the swing roll, is the same as the forward outside swing roll, which you learned in Chapter Three as a part of freestyle skating. In ice dancing, it's called a swing roll.

The Dutch Waltz has three swing rolls in it. All are done on the outside edge.

The swing roll starts on the first count of music. Your free foot swings forward on the fourth count of music. (Although the music is in 3/4 time, skaters count one-two-three-four-five-six, rather than one-two-three-one-two-three.)

The Dutch Waltz pattern is based on eight steps done two times around the rink on eight alternating lobes. Remember that a lobe is a half-circle, so you only have eight steps to memorize. After doing the eight steps two times, you will be back where you started on the ice.

In the eight steps you will learn, there are only three different moves:

1. The three-step progressive
2. The swing roll (which you have already learned)
3. The corner step

The Progressive Step

The progressive step in ice dancing can either be a two-step progressive or a three-step progressive. The Dutch Waltz uses only a three-step progressive.

The FO, FI, and FO edges make up your progressive step.

As the name implies, the step should "progress" or move ahead. It should start and end on a lobe.

The Swing Roll

You will be doing a swing roll on your outside edge. The free foot will swing forward on beat number four of the six beats of the swing roll lobe. This dance has three swing rolls. Can you see them in the dance diagram? They are number 2, 3 and 7. If you identified them, you are beginning to read figure skating choreography.

Tip: If you want to do the Dutch Waltz, you'll first memorize the steps. When you're skating, you will be concentrating on how to do each step, as well as anticipating the next step. Learn them well so you can enjoy the smooth movement of the dance and the pleasure of skating with your partner.

The Corner Step

The corner step is the easiest; it is also called the edge step. There is a corner step in each of the four corners of the rink. It is always a LFO, followed by a RFI. Each step is three beats. Look at the diagram again and you will see these notations.

After the introduction, the steps of the Dutch Waltz go like this:

1. LFO, RFI, LFO progressive
2. RFO swing roll
3. LFO swing roll
4. RFO, LFI, RFO progressive
5. LFO, RFI corner step
6. LFO, RFI, LFO progressive
7. RFO Swing roll
8. LFO, RFI corner step

To complete the dance, you'll repeat these eight steps. Practice the pattern while skating alone until you have memorized the pattern and feel comfortable with the steps. Are you ready to start your first ice dance? Find a partner.

> **Tip:** If you run out of space, then your lobes are not tight enough. Bend more to make tighter lobes. Have fun!

In the middle of the rink

- Stand still in a "T" position with your partner. The girl is on her partner's right side in the kilian position.
- Face one end of the rink.
- Her left shoulder is in front, touching his right shoulder.
- Her left arm is extended in front of him.
- His right arm is across her back.
- His right hand and her right hand are together, and securely on her right hip.
- Both members of the dance team (that's what you are called now) will push onto their left feet as the first of three introductory steps.
- Do three forward strokes with considerable power. The three strokes will be RFI, LFI, RFI.
- You should reach the starting point of the dance by the end of your third stroke.
- Follow the eight steps of the dance.
- Repeat them until you end up where you started.

General hints for ice dancing:

- Always bring your feet together after each step sequence.
- Bend deeply *before* each step.
- Look where you are going.

- Agree with your partner as to who will follow and who will lead.
- Both partners should first be guided by the music, not by each other.

There are about twenty ice dances. You have learned the first one. After you feel you are doing the Dutch Waltz reasonably well, you will probably want to learn some of the other dances. You might even invent a new one!

PART TWO

FOR INTERMEDIATE (ONCE-A-WEEK) SKATERS

CHAPTER EIGHT

Moving On

This section of the book is directed to intermediate skaters—those who have decided to skate regularly, once a week or more. As before, the main objectives will be having fun and improving basic skills.

Intermediate skating is a relative term. It varies, depending on where you skate. If you are at a rink that doesn't have a professional staff, you may be the best skater . . . yet you are really still an intermediate skater. On the other hand, if you learn to skate at one of the international training sites, it's going to take you a long time to reach the intermediate level. When you're ready to call yourself an intermediate skater, it is time to buy new skates—and maybe a special outfit, just for skating.

Buying Skates for the Intermediate Skater

If you are going to skate once a week or more, you will need better skates than the ones you bought or rented as a beginner. When you shop for new skates, wear the same kind of socks that you will wear for skating. Thin cotton socks are best. Your new skates will be heavier than your starter skates, which probably had one or two layers of leather. Intermediate-level boots will have three or four or more pieces of leather. Some boots, for high-level skaters, can have nine pieces of leather in them. Each layer adds weight. Your new blades will be made of harder and better quality steel. They will not be nickel-plated.

To start, try on a size or two smaller than your shoe size. Lace the toe area, being sure to pull the tongue up. Then lace the middle area tightly for ankle support, and the top area loosely so that you can bend properly. (You may want to review the instructions for lacing in Chapter One.)

When you stand, bend so that your knees are over your toes when you look down. To test the fit of your boots, review pages 22–26 and check the following points:

Toe area: Your toes should be able to wiggle up and down, but not curl under. They shouldn't move from side to side and they shouldn't feel like a hand is pinching your toes together.

Ankle area: The ankle should feel like a strong hand is clasping it. Your arch should feel supported. You shouldn't have to use your leg muscles to keep your ankle supported. Supporting your ankle is the skate's job, not yours. When you bend even deeper, your feet should feel some resistance from the boots, but not pain. Your toes should spread out in the boot as you bend deeply.

Heel area: Your heel should be planted into the socket of the boot. Stand on one foot, while supporting your balance by holding on to something. Kick the other foot out, making sure your heel doesn't move within the boot. If it does, you will have difficulty on your jumps.

These skates will be used for learning new jumps. They must be strong enough to support you as you take off and land. If you are satisfied with the fit, the support, and the flexibility, you then have the right skates for intermediate skating.

New Blades

As an intermediate skater, you will buy your blades separately from your boots. Your new blades will be mounted to the bottoms of your boots with screws. They will be placed carefully for your individual balance.

The blade you choose will depend on whether you plan to

do freestyle, synchronized team skating, or ice dancing. Ice dancing requires a shorter blade, and the heel of the blade does not protrude beyond the boot as far as other blades. The toe picks of an ice-dancing blade are less pronounced than those on freestyle blades. That's because in freestyle skating, you need your toe picks to grip the ice securely as you take off or land a jump. The blades used in synchronized team skating combine elements of both the ice-dancing blade and the freestyle blade, because synchronized skaters do moves associated with both types of skating. The choices are up to each individual.

On average, the blade will be about nine inches long. You will decide if you want a long radius or a short radius. The radius measures the curvature of the blade from toe to heel. The radius of this measurement varies from six-and-a-half feet to eight feet. A good choice is a seven-foot radius, with a three-eighth-inch hollow to the sharpness of the blade.

A seven-foot radius is good for spinning, yet it gives enough contact with the ice for secure takeoffs and landings of jumps. The seven-sixteenths- to three-eighths-of-an-inch hollow is comfortable for intermediate skaters. Try seven-sixteenths first. This number represents the diameter of the sharpening tool that is used to create the hollow area that runs down the length of your blade, between the edges. Your new blades will be of quality steel, will hold a sharpening well, and will give you a good grip as you take off for a jump.

Breaking in New Boots

Everyone agrees that breaking in new boots can be time-consuming and painful. But experts disagree on how to make the process easier. Here are some suggestions:

- Allow six to eight hours of practice time for breaking in new boots. Start with short sessions, a half-hour at most, and build gradually to your usual practice time.

- Many skaters time their purchases so they can break in new boots in the summer, before the competition season starts.

- Begin breaking in new boots off the ice. Wear the skates, including the boots, blades, and blade guards, at home. Walk around with your knees and ankles well bent. Do not walk in the boots without blades, as you may distort the metal shank that keeps the boot rigid.

- At first, don't lace the top pair of hooks.

- On the ice, do back crossovers in both directions. Because this move requires deeply bent knees and ankles, it is the most efficient way to create flexibility in the boot. Postpone jumping until you feel your alignment is comfortable on all edges.

- Do not go back to your old boots, even if the new ones are presenting a challenge. Once you have new boots, keep breaking them in.

- You can ask the staff at your pro shop, where you bought the boots, to punch out the ankles or other tight spots. Some boot specialists will ask you to point out on your bare foot the places that hurt. They mark the trouble spots with lipstick, then you put your boot on and the lipstick rubs off on the lining of the boot, showing the expert where you need more room.

- Wear knee-high socks instead of waist-high tights while breaking in new boots. When you remove your skates, take off your socks and examine your feet. Look for red spots or blisters so you can have the boots adjusted before a small injury becomes more serious.

- The "wet sock treatment" has a lot of fans. They believe that if you wet a pair of socks and put them on your feet, towel them dry so they are not dripping, then put your new boots on for at least a half-hour, your body will warm

> **Tip:** When you buy new boots, allow plenty of time to break them in before a competition, test, or skating event. No one can skate well with boots that are not broken in.

the moisture in the socks, and that in turn will soften the leather so that it molds to fit your foot. This is best done on the ice, not at home. True, your feet will feel cold for a short time, but this technique can shorten the break-in period enough to make it worthwhile.

- Make a note of how long it takes you to break in your new boots, so that in the future you will know how much time to allow.

- After your boots are broken in, remember always to undo your laces enough so that you don't force your foot into the boot. You'll be breaking down the boot, which means you'll have to buy new ones sooner than you would like and no one wants to break in boots sooner than is necessary.

- Replace your laces regularly, not just when they break. Old laces stretch, compromising their ability to support. In addition, they can make a dent in the tongue, which makes it difficult for you to lace your boots tightly enough.

Mounting of Your Blades

Now that you have your boots in one hand and your blades in the other (don't let the edges touch one another), you are ready to have your blades mounted.

The standard placement of blades is slightly to the inside of the center axis of the boot. If you are knock-kneed or under-weight, the placement of the blades will be closer to the center axis or even toward the outside of the boot. If you are bowlegged or overweight, the placement will be toward the inside or almost on the center axis of the sole of the boot. The back part of the blade is usually just a bit to the inside of the center of the heel.

The balance has to feel right to you. When you skate on one foot, with your body in a neutral position, you should feel no resistance. Your tracing should be a straight line. Try this on each foot both forward and backward.

SYNCHRONIZED TEAM SKATING

Synchronized team skating is also called precision or ensemble skating. All these terms mean skating together at the same time, in unison. It is an ideal activity for an intermediate skater who enjoys working with others. Team skaters impress audiences with their complicated steps, their power and speed, and the beauty of the patterns made by eight to twenty-four talented skaters.

Besides performing during the intermissions at hockey games—like cheerleaders at football games—team skaters also compete.

Synchronized skating is a real team sport. If one skater in a line is slightly off, or can't remember his or her steps, the judges penalize the whole team. The skaters learn not only to smile as they skate, but also to talk to one another as they smile and skate. The audience will never hear their comments, such as "Karen, slow down!"

Synchronized skating has been around since the beginning of the century, but it wasn't until 1960 that it became organized. It has increased in popularity since the days when it was like a marching band on ice, without instruments, sometimes with a kick line thrown in.

There are two tiers or levels of synchronized skating: recreational and competitive. In areas where the sport is popular, there are synchronized skating teams for different age levels, as well as all-boy and all-girl teams.

Synchronized skating teams do creative moves, based on long edges. Marching on ice is a thing of the past. Competitions include both short and long programs, lasting from two minutes, forty seconds up to four minutes, thirty seconds. The music is sophisticated and lively. Lifts have recently been allowed in competitions. Synchronized skaters have become quite innovative.

Synchronized skaters start off by buying ready-made costumes. The costumes are made from a stretch fabric, like spandex, and are chosen to bring out the meaning of the music. For example, if you are skating to *Swan Lake*, you and your team would wear white outfits. If "Rhapsody in Blue" is your music, you might choose to skate in medium blue costumes, with silver trim.

Skaters must be careful when choosing a hairstyle for performances. Coaches do not allow any ribbons or bobby pins to be used. The risk of these items falling on the ice and tripping another skater is too high.

Hair falling across the eyes, even momentarily, could cause the skater to use her hand to push it aside. This is distracting when a soloist does it, but it's a major error when a member of a synchronized team does it. Choose a hairstyle that holds your hair close to your head if it is long, and a style that doesn't need hair accessories if it is short.

ONCE-A-WEEK SKATERS

Tip: If you are interested in doing synchronized team skating, you will need to be well trained, well groomed, and well polished. Just as you will do skating moves in unison with your teammates, you will also wear the same costumes, hairstyles, and makeup.

Coaches of synchronized skating teams are usually former team members, either in qualifying competitions or in professional ice shows. More often than not, they act as both the coach and the choreographer.

Although synchronized skating is not yet an Olympic sport, it has started the procedure to qualify. If you are interested in synchronized team skating, check with your pro as to where and when it is done in your area.

SKATING CLUBS AND ASSOCIATIONS

Skating Clubs

There are two types of skating clubs. One kind is run by the rink, and its emphasis is on group lessons. The other is a private club, run by volunteers, with the focus on social, uncrowded practice sessions and general group lessons. As an intermediate skater, look for the club that will match your objectives: having fun and improving. In most cases, a private club will offer you the most benefits, unless you skate at one of the top training centers.

Skating Associations

Figure skating has two main skating associations: the ISI (Ice Skating Institute) and the USFSA (United States Figure Skating Association).

Most skaters join the ISI first. It is not necessary to join any association unless you are interested in testing and/or competitions. If you want to start taking achievement tests, I recommend joining the ISI.

Instructors

There are three terms for instructors:

- A teacher instructs in safety concerns and basic moves— forward skating, stopping, and forward crossovers.

Tip: Whether you take occasional lessons as a beginner, one lesson a week as an intermediate skater, or many lessons a week as a serious skater, you should have the same objective: to memorize how your body feels while your instructor is teaching. If you remind yourself of this so that it becomes a habit, you will be pleased with your quick progress and what great benefits you get from your lessons.

- A pro, or professional, usually teaches intermediate skaters, and the lessons are usually once a week. A pro can be helpful in advising students about buying skates and improving their skating techniques and choosing a coach.

- A coach does many things. Mainly, he or she coaches correcting very technical moves. A coach works with competitors, attends competitions, and is highly rated by the PSA, the Professional Skaters Association. A coach advises skaters about costumes, makeup, music, skates, blades, mounting, sharpenings, nutrition, supplementary exercises, confidence, and training schedules. He or she supplies hand holding, tear wiping, and hugs. A coach charges more than a teacher or a pro.

LESSONS

Group lessons are great when the all the students are at the same level and you have an inspiring, knowledgeable pro. As you improve, you will want more individual attention. At that point you may want to consider taking some private lessons. Although private lessons are more expensive, you can learn faster by having your individual needs addressed.

Workshops are somewhat new to figure skating. They have

proven to be very successful. Specialists in various fields, such as forward skating, basic turns, or spinning, offer the workshops, often with an assistant to help out. Some workshops give general instruction in choreography, audience appeal, makeup, or off-ice training. Workshops may be held for a few hours in one day or may take place over a few days. Some have as few as four students, while a stroking workshop with an internationally respected coach can have over fifty. Workshops can be more expensive than private lessons, but many students feel that, dollar for dollar, the workshop is well worth its price. If you choose a workshop carefully according to your ability and the coach, you'll gain a lot.

CHOOSING AN INSTRUCTOR

Whether you choose a teacher, a pro, or a coach of figure skating, you should expect your instructor to work hard with you to get the most improvement based on your time for practice. Instructors respect students regardless of their level of commitment. That doesn't mean that they won't especially encourage a student who they feel has talent to consider serious skating.

In choosing an instructor, be frank about your goals as a skater. Does the instructor understand them? Consider them realistic? Have other goals to suggest? Most important, does he or she really understand that you want to enjoy as well as improve your skating?

SKATING COMPETITIONS

Both the ISI and the USFSA now have a similar basic achievement test structure, and both associations hold qualifying and nonqualifying competitions. The big difference is that only through the USFSA can you qualify to compete in the most prestigious of all competitions, the Olympics, which are held every four years. For this reason, most skaters start with the ISI and then move over to the USFSA.

In order to compete in qualifying competitions sanctioned by the USFSA, you must be either an individual member of the USFSA or a member of a USFSA club. Through the USFSA you will be introduced to testing, from the pre-preliminary test all the way up to the senior level. Serious skaters will need to pass these tests to compete in qualifying competitions, perhaps all the way to the highest competition, the Olympics.

SUMMER CAMPS FOR SKATING

Many skaters find that summers are a great time to improve their skating skills. The long break from school provides an opportunity to spend more time on the ice. There are roughly a thousand summer skating programs throughout North America, including camps that are devoted to the training of high-level competitors and Olympians. Camp sessions may range from two weeks to the full summer in length.

If you are a first-timer at skating camp, you may want to start at a two-week camp that is not too far from your home. Chances are you'll know some of the other skaters attending the camp. Later, you will feel more comfortable with a longer camp session and longer distances.

Here are some questions to ask when you're exploring summer camp options:

- Does the camp offer other activities, such as gymnastics, dance, weight training, nutrition counseling, and sports psychology, that can enhance your skating?

- How many rinks does the camp have? Are all of them available for figure skating? What is the schedule?

- Does the camp offer skaters the chance to perform in exhibitions on a regular schedule?

ONCE-A-WEEK SKATERS

- Does the camp offer testing?
- What are the housing arrangements? Typically, they may range from dormitories to boarding houses.
- What are the credentials of the pros who teach there, and how do you schedule your time with them?
- What are the ages of the skaters who attend, and what is the biggest age group?
- Can the camp refer you to other skaters who have attended past sessions, so you can talk to them and find out their opinions?

Choose the features that are most important to you. Of course, as with all aspects of skating, you will need to discuss the costs and benefits with your parents. Many skaters feel they make more progress during summer than during the nine months of the school year.

PART THREE

FOR SERIOUS SKATERS

CHAPTER NINE

I Think I Have Talent—What's Next?

If you think you have talent, go for it! Develop it, nurture it, and see how far it will take you. You will never regret becoming a better skater. You will only regret if you don't try.

How do you know if you have talent? You just know it. It's an inner feeling. Even if you're not right, you will not have made the wrong decision in pursuing your dream. You can still achieve your two objectives: to enjoy skating and to improve.

If you keep things in perspective, you can only succeed. After years of being tested and judged in competition, years of great fun, years of having made great friends, years of traveling and learning more about yourself through this great sport, you are going to be a better person!

KEEPING THINGS IN PERSPECTIVE

Every parent, every friend, every brother or sister, every skater has great hindsight. They see each skater start out the same way: He or she likes the idea of skating, and wants to learn it. Before long the skater wants to become better, then to test and compete. And before you know it, he or she feels like a star, and wants that Olympic gold medal.

The odds of winning the gold medal in Olympics are pretty long: there is only one winner in each discipline every four years. Even if the odds are in your favor, you could come down with the flu, or suffer a stress fracture, or run into another last-minute problem. It's not a good idea to have the gold medal in Olympics as your ultimate goal at the beginning of your skating. Aim to enjoy skating and please yourself instead.

HOW TO SAVE MONEY AND TIME

If you are going to compete in skating, you need to understand what steps you have to take. Experience is your best teacher. You will learn as you go along.

Here are a few tips to help you:

- Join a club that holds tests and supports competitive skaters. Some skating clubs sponsor up-and-coming competitors.

- Enroll in the USFSA official test structure. (This is different from the USFSA basic tests.)

- Hire the best coach you can find, preferably one who is rated by the PSA. Your coach should have a track record of success with competitive skaters and judges, and his or her personality should be compatible with yours.

- Make sure you have plenty of ice time for practice, either through your rink, or through a local skating club.

- Get advice and help in choosing the right boots and blades.

- Arrange for some off-ice supplementary fitness training. Ask your coach to help you figure out what you will need.

- Work on flexibility, power, endurance, strength, agility, and maintenance training.

- Get the proper amount of rest for your training schedule.

- Eat a healthful diet—consistently! If you are eating food that is usually sold at the rink (pizzas, hot dogs, sodas), your body will need better fuel. Top skaters work with nutritionists to make sure they are getting the most from what they eat.

- On a regular basis, talk to your parents about what skating costs—in money, in effort, and in the attention that it demands. It is important to discuss the effects on the rest of your family.

CHOOSING A COACH

Choosing a coach for private lessons is a big step. Your relationship with your coach can last through competitions, professional skating, and retirement; it can be a lifetime friendship. On the other hand, you may have a number of coaches who help you, even though they teach and train differently. It is difficult to pick the right one at the beginning, but these guidelines should help you.

- The larger the skating facility is, the wider the choice of coaches will be.
- Do you prefer a male or a female authority figure? Give this plenty of thought, not only for the immediate years, but also for the years ahead.
- Do you do better with a nurturing type or a strict disciplinarian? You can expect both to be firm; it's just that their style of delivery is different. Their style must motivate you.
- Check out each coach's qualifications. Coaches belong to professional associations. The most popular, and the one that most rinks require their staffs to join, is the PSA, The Professional Skaters Association. The PSA rating system is based not only on what the coach did as a skater before turning professional, but also on how successful his or her students have been, since then. The rating system goes

SERIOUS
SKATERS

from certified to a master's level. Most highly successful coaches have master ratings from the PSA.

- You must feel comfortable with your coach. Developing a rapport becomes very important.
- When you choose a coach, you should have a gut feeling that "this is going to work." Both you and your coach will be investing a lot of effort.

WHAT TO EXPECT FROM A COACH

Every coach is different; each one has strong points and weak points—just like skaters.

- Your coach should help you with buying new skates and blades. (Naturally, you should do your homework so you're well informed and know your preferences beforehand.)
- A coach should guide you in your choice of skating music.
- Coaches should inform all students which competitions they will attend with their students. Some coaches will only go to a competition if they have a certain number of students.
- Above all, you need open and free communication with your coach.

WHAT YOUR COACH EXPECTS FROM YOU

Once you have made a commitment to study with a coach, you have certain responsibilities.

- Start by having a doctor check you out with a physical exam. Explain the training schedule you intend to keep.
- About one in ten women skaters have an eating disorder. Boys are subject to eating disorders, also. Be honest with your doctor. The doctor will check your height-weight ratio and will discuss your eating habits.

- Be consistent in your conditioning regimen. Get enough sleep on a consistent basis. Train, but do not over-train. Participate in off-ice supplementary practice as your coach sees fit.

- Work with your coach in selecting music. It is vital that you love the music you choose for your skating program. You will hear it over and over, so liking your music is not good enough . . . you must *love* your music.

- Just as you expect your coach to talk openly with you, make sure you are frank with your coach.

How to Get the Most from Your Lessons

You have a big challenge as a student—memorizing how your body feels in doing the moves as your coach has described, so that you always practice them correctly. By doing so, you will develop muscle memory and make the best use of your practice. A lot of skaters do "mindless practice," just throwing jumps, spins, and arm movements around. Be aware of your moves so you can ask your coach intelligent questions about perfecting them.

Approach each lesson with a goal in mind.

You and your coach will discuss immediate and long-range goals. Every lesson should have a purpose. Coaches often will ask their students to write out their goals at the beginning of a season. If your coach doesn't ask you to do this, you can do it on your own. Some skaters write out their goals for each lesson, each practice session, each week, each month, each season.

You are responsible for being prepared and ready ahead of your lesson time. Hiring a coach is a commitment of your effort, and your parents' money. When you come to your lesson, make sure you are properly dressed, your skates are laced correctly, and your laces are tucked in.

SERIOUS SKATERS

The Role of Your Parents

Most coaches will make time to speak to a parent when the occasion arises—and this includes if the skater is losing interest. Often kids are very enthusiastic in the beginning, but then they lose interest, or they want to use the time another way. It's easy for a parent to recognize that a child wants to make a commitment. Recognizing that he or she has had enough is harder. Always make every effort to explain your feelings to your parents.

Skating associations publish rulebooks every year. Show the books to your parents. It is important to have the most recent rulebook of the skating associations to which you belong. Find time to discuss the rules with your parents.

You will have some frustrating and discouraging times in your skating career. You may cry, and that's hard for your parents to take. Sometimes, you will feel that the coach is making unreasonable demands. If you need help, talk to your parents about the problem. Maybe they will want to talk with your coach—or maybe they won't. Some parents like to be involved in every aspect of their children's lives. Other parents have a "hands off" attitude and want their child to handle things. Understand how your parents feel about this and know what is your responsibility.

Boots: Custom-Made vs. Store-Bought

Custom-made boots are "made to measure" and store-bought boots are "made to fit." There are only a few dozen "hand" boot makers in the world. Of those, only six in North America specialize in ice skate boots. Some will do all the measuring by computer. The others do the measuring with a very skilled and experienced hand. All feel strongly that their method is the best. Custom-made boots are expensive (around $600)—and they can take about six weeks to make. You would think that with this amount of patience and this amount of money, all clients would be 100 percent satisfied. Sorry, but not everyone is happy with their custom-made skates. It's no one's fault; it's just an imperfect science.

Many top skaters today buy good-quality skate boots "off the rack" or stock skates and bring them to a skilled repairman to stretch, punch, pull, and hammer the leather according to the skater's wishes. Skaters who do this know exactly what they are looking for in the fit of their boot and they find this method gives them good results. Buying skates "off the rack" and then adapting them is also good for someone who wants to get the new skates quickly. In the long run, this approach is usually less expensive than getting custom-made boots.

If you buy skates "off the rack," take along your old pair. The blade might be the right size and have enough good steel in it to be used on the new boot. Also, the old boots will show the stress points. An experienced sales person can use that information to help you choose the right skates for your skating level.

MOUNTING AND SHARPENING OF BLADES

Your coach will advise you about the mounting and sharpening of your blades, but here are some guidelines, so you'll understand the process.

When we say a blade is mounted, we mean that it is attached to the bottom of the skate boot with screws. The placement of the blade is very important.

Generally, when the blade is placed on the bottom of the boot, the front end of it is placed almost flush with the toe of

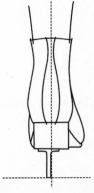

Mounting of blades for the serious skater

the boot. The heel of the blade will nearly reach the end of the boot heel. An experienced person who mounts skates can look at the boot and the blade to decide what size blade to use. Basically, you want the blade to be parallel to the centerline of the sole of the boot, and about one-eighth of an inch to the inside of the center line.

Blades have twelve screw holes. When your blades are attached, they will be set in a temporary mounting, with only four or six screws used. The temporary mounting allows you to test the placement of the blades on the ice. Do not attempt to do jumps with a temporary mounting, as the screws may come loose. Your coach may help you test the placement. Some skaters prefer slightly different mountings on each skate. Our bodies are not symmetrical!

It may take several sessions to decide if you are happy with the first mounting. During this time, make sure you are doing all edges, both forward and backward, and at all different speeds. If you are not happy with the mounting, explain in detail where you feel uncomfortable. Don't be too quick to decide.

There is a disadvantage in having the blade remounted: Every time a screw hole is placed in the sole of the boot, you are shortening the life of the boot. Moisture can get into these holes. The sole of the boot is made of leather, or in some cases, of cork. The moisture entering the sole eats away at the material. The life of the boot decreases. Because no one enjoys breaking in new boots, we want our boots to last as long as possible. Blades usually last longer than boots.

Sharpening

A sharpener grinds out the hollow between the two edges of your blade to make it deeper and blends in any nicks in the steel. Blades must be sharp in order to grip the ice. You would

General Guidelines for Sharpening

One-half inch for beginners or occasional skaters

Seven-sixteenths-inch hollow for intermediate skaters or once-a-week skaters

Three-eighths for serious skaters or every day skaters

The measurements one-half, seven-sixteenths, or three-eighths of an inch refer to the radius of the cylinder tool that your blade sharpener uses.

think that when you buy new blades, they would be sharp. Right? Wrong! The new blade has to be sharpened before you use it. They are made this way because, at this level, skaters want different sharpenings. If you are not experienced in choosing a hollow, have your blade sharpened at a three-eighths-of-an-inch hollow.

If you are skating several times a week, your sharpening may last about six months. Keep a record of your sharpenings. You'll want to remember when it was done, who did it, what size hollow was used, and how long it took after the sharpening date before you adjusted and felt comfortable again on your blades.

Your sharpening record is helpful when you are tested, or when you compete. Before the test or competition date, you can have your blades sharpened by someone you trust, and because you kept a record, you will know what to expect for the important day.

SERIOUS
SKATERS

PART FOUR

FOR FANS OF SKATING

CHAPTER TEN

HOW TO BE AN INFORMED FAN

The world of skaters needs fans! Whether you are watching from your couch in your living room or bringing your autograph book to every skating show and competition, your support keeps skating going, and the skating stars that perform for you appreciate your support and enthusiasm.

Figure skating on television is a lot more interesting after you've seen a live performance, but there's an advantage to watching skating on television: the commentators will help teach you to recognize the different jumps. Even for experienced skaters, it is sometimes difficult to tell the difference between a triple jump and a quadruple jump. Commentators are very helpful.

To educate yourself as a spectator, concentrate on recognizing the different kinds of jumps before trying to recognize the number of rotations. Even television commentators occasionally make mistakes in counting the number of rotations! Jumps are roughly divided into edge jumps and toe-assisted jumps. The difference is in the takeoff. The axel, double axel, and triple axel (very rare) have a forward takeoff. The other jumps—loops, salchows, flips, lutzes, toe loops, and walleys—all have a backward takeoff. When the jumps are shown in slow motion, concentrate on the takeoff edge. It can be forward, or backward, and with or without the toe for assistance.

FANS OF
SKATING

173

SKATING SHOWS AT YOUR LOCAL ARENA

Skating shows are a thrill for the spectator. The performers have a good time, too. In shows, they are more relaxed than when they compete. They really hear the appreciation of their fans. They often choose music to which the audience can clap.

If you want to take photographs at a skating show, do not use flashbulbs. The sudden light can be very disturbing and even dangerous to the performers. The lighting in arenas is such that you will be happy with your non-flash photos.

If you personally know a performer, get in touch with him or her *before* the show. He or she can arrange for you to get past security before or after the show, but your visit must be planned well in advance. The security surrounding today's skating stars is, of necessity, strong.

If you want to get an autograph or photo of your favorite skater, write to him or her in care of the skating show. This address is listed in the skating program. You can also contact the stars through the show's Web site. Most skaters are glad to handle the autographs this way. Save all your programs of skating shows. It will be interesting to look through them in the future.

The first time you see live performances of skating stars, you will be amazed at how fast they cover the ice. When they are being filmed for television, their speed doesn't really come across. The television camera often moves with the skater, so you are not aware of the skater covering 180 feet at about twenty-two miles per hour.

LIVE COMPETITIONS

Attending competitions is more serious than following skating shows. Competitions decide who is going to claim or reclaim a title, and who the new up-and-coming stars will be.

Did you know that you can buy tickets to see the skaters in their practice sessions? The practice-session tickets are not as expensive as the ones for the competition, and the practice sessions are often much more exciting. More unexpected things happen, and you get a feeling about the personalities of the skaters. As in skating shows, don't take flash photos. Do not make noise or change your seat while a skater is performing. Wait until the music ends before making any move.

If you plan to bring flowers or stuffed animals to your favorite skater, make sure they are wrapped in plastic. (If you purchase them at the skating rink, they will be in plastic.) Imagine if you were a skating star, performing all over the United States and parts of Canada. Imagine all the flowers and stuffed animals you could get. You'd line your hotel room with them. Soon you would have so many flowers and animals in your room that you could hardly find your bed. What would you do with all those gifts from your fans? Take them with you to the show's next city? Send them back? Or, send them to the local hospital? The last is correct: that is just what the skaters do.

The best seat to try to get for a skating competition is right behind the judges. The second best seat is across the rink from the judges. If you get seats high up in the back of the arena, make sure you bring binoculars. You can alternate between watching the skater's overall program from a distance and, with the binoculars, seeing their costumes, tracings, and expressions up close.

Don't be late for the short or long program. The order of the short program is determined by a random draw. The best skater may be first. The long program has five or six skaters to a group. Although the best skaters skate toward the end, it is considered rude to show up once the long program has started. You may spot an up-and-coming skater who is not yet ranked high. It is fun to follow this skater over the years, and say, "I spotted her way back, when she was a kid, and I knew she had it."

FANS OF
SKATING

Another fun thing to do at competitions is pretend that you are a judge. You will be judging both the technical merit and the presentation of each performance. In your technical marks you will want to consider:

- How many different moves your skater does.
- How confidently these moves are performed.
- The difficulty of the chosen moves.

In judging presentation you will want to look for:

- How well the whole ice surface is covered.
- How well the music is expressed by the skater.
- How fast and powerful the skater remains throughout the program. (Skaters often slow down on the last half-minute of skating. A well-trained skater can keep the same pace all the way through.)
- The tracings: If you saw the tracings as a painting, would it be interesting? Would it be balanced? Do the tracings go both directions, clockwise and counterclockwise? Give lower marks to the skater who favors one direction.

Pretending to be a judge makes you appreciate how much credit the judges in skating deserve. It's hard to judge!

In qualifying competitions, the competitors are striving for the gold medal of the Winter Olympics. If you are a follower of competitions, this is the competition you will enjoy the most. It is the most expensive, and probably the most inconvenient to attend, but it is the most exciting, so make plans to attend if at all possible.

CHAPTER ELEVEN

I Don't Skate, but I Want to Be Involved

Even if you don't skate, you can find a place in the world of figure skating. Many people are surprised to learn that the judges of figure-skating tests and competitions are not necessarily figure skaters themselves.

- Did you ever think of all the related professionals who are involved in skating? The talents range from acupuncturists to Zamboni engineers.

- Did you know that former skaters as well as non-skaters design the beautiful costumes?

- Did you know that all skating competitions depend on volunteers? This goes from the smallest competitions to the Olympics. If you speak more than one language, you will be welcome at international competitions, including the Olympics.

If you spend time at skating rinks and among skaters, you may meet—and perhaps think about helping—a hard-working skater who can't afford the costs of skating. This is where sponsors come in. Sponsors are people who want to help others.

It isn't just the figure-skating performer that makes this sport. There are "angels" behind the scenes and in the wings.

HELP WANTED: VOLUNTEERS

When local skating clubs sponsor competitions, they must follow the rules and regulations of skating associations. They need help in organizing their events. If you want to volunteer, contact the chairperson of your local skating club. You will learn a lot, and you'll be contributing a lot.

DESIGNING SKATING COSTUMES

Most rinks have a pro shop where you can buy standard practice and competitive costumes. Most rinks also have someone who does more and better costumes than the pro shop. Often, these are mothers of skaters or even non-skaters. They start by making a practice show or competitive costume. They get compliments, then they get orders. There is no age requirement. Sometimes ten-year-olds design their own costumes.

Skating costumes for both men and women must be made of stretch fabric. The costume has to be designed so that the trim doesn't drop onto the ice and cause someone to fall. It must be comfortable, and when you lift your arms, as skaters do, the costume can't hike up.

One of today's best designers is Vera Wang of New York City. Ms. Wang is a former figure skater and competitor. Who knows better about having comfort in a dress than a former skater?

HAPPY SKATING!

Figure skating can be many things to many people. If you want to be comfortable and skate a few times a season, bring out your trusty recreational skates that feel like sneakers on your feet, and make a few turns around the ice.

If you want to explore basic skating as a single skater, practice pairs or ice dancing moves with a partner, or get together with a precision team on a weekly schedule, you can do that, with a quality pair of skates.

If you are a serious skater and can commit to skating every day, you'll buy custom or high-end skates, arrange for proper coaching, and join the ranks of skating stars who never gave up their dream of gliding across the ice on one silver blade, head up and arms outstretched.

Even if you are a non-skater/spectator rather than a skater, remember that you, too, can be part of the skating world. Your talent, backstage help, applause, and enthusiasm can make a huge contribution to the world of figure skating.

Whatever your interest level, and whatever your age, skating has something to offer you, and you have something to offer the skating world!

FANS OF SKATING

GLOSSARY OF SKATING TERMS

Arabesque (sometimes called a spiral): A position in which the skater balances on one foot, with the other leg extended backward, higher than the skater's head.

Axel: A freestyle jump of one-and-a-half rotations. The takeoff edge is forward.

Axis: An imaginary line connecting two points.

Beginner or **starter:** Someone who skates occasionally.

Blade: The silver-metal runner that is attached to the sole of the skate boot.

Blade guards: Plastic or rubber covers that protect blades from being damaged.

Boot: The leather part of the skate that is laced, or, in a recreational skate, is tightened. Usually white for girls, black for boys.

Centered spin: A spin that has tracings that are in one spot. The opposite of a centered spin is a traveled spin.

Centrifugal force: The pull outward when a skater is rotating rapidly around a center. For example: your arms, hair, and clothing pull out when spinning.

Cheated jump: A jump in which the skater has not completed the rotation in the air, but on the ice. (An error. No one intends to cheat a jump.)

Check, checking: To rotate the body against the direction of the skating edge.

Choreography: Planned skating moves that match the music in sound and in spirit.

Clean ice: Ice that doesn't have any tracings on it. Freshly resurfaced ice.

Coach: An instructor of serious students.

Corner step: An ice dance term, also called the corner step. In the Dutch Waltz, it is two steps of three beats each.

Crossovers: A skating move, done forward and backward, to increase speed by crossing one foot over the other onto a new edge.

Custom-made skates: Skates that are made to fit your foot.

Death spiral: A pair move in which the woman's body is parallel to the ice. Her partner holds her by one hand as he stabilizes the move by bending low and balancing on one toe and one blade.

Diameter: A measure from one side of a circle through the center to the other side of the circle.

Dirty ice: Ice with tracings on it. Also called used ice.

Dutch Waltz: A basic ice dance of eight steps, done forward in a kilian position.

Edge (as in blade): Each blade has two edges. They are about one-eighth of an inch apart.

Edge (as in stroke): A curved tracing, also called a swing roll, or a lobe. It is done by balancing on one foot and one edge.

Ensemble skating: Also called synchronized or precision skating. Usually done by eight to twenty-four skaters.

Flat: When both the inner and the outer edge are on the ice. The tracing will show two parallel lines about one-eighth of an inch apart.

Flip: A jump of one rotation taking off from a back inside edge.

Flutz: A combination of the flip and a lutz. As the skater takes off for her lutz, she carelessly lets her takeoff edge go from a back outside edge to a back inside edge. Judges mark this with low marks.

Free foot, free arm, free side, etc.: If the skater is on the right foot, the left side of the body is the free side, and vice-versa. Hence the free foot, free arm, etc.

Hockey stop: A stop done by turning and scraping all edges.

Hollow: The concave area of the bottom of the blades, between the two edges.

Honing stone: A small stone that one uses to gently remove nicks on a blade.

Hydroplaning: When two skaters (four blades) are totally supported by one blade. Terrific speed, lean, and edge quality are needed.

Ice dancing: A team of two skaters who have restrictions and limits on their small lifts and jumps.

Instructor/teacher: An instructor of figure skating who starts beginners in basic moves and safety rules.

Intermediate: One who skates frequently (at least once a week).

ISI: The Ice Skating Institute: An association that oversees starter tests and competitions.

ISU: The International Skating Union. An organization that governs both figure skating and speed skating at World and Olympic competitions.

Kilian position: An ice dance hold. The woman is to the right of the man, as both skate forward.

Kiss-and-cry area: At an important competition, television cameras are always here to record what the skaters, and coaches do: kiss and cry.

LFO: Left forward outer edge.

LFI: Left forward inner edge.

LBO: Left back outer edge.

LBI: Left back inner edge.

LFF: Left forward flat.

LBF: Left back flat.

Lobe: An ice dance term. A curved tracing that is similar to a half-circle shape.

Long program: The last part of the singles and the pairs competition.

Lutz: A jump of one rotation taking off from a back outside edge.

Mirror skating: The tracings of the two skaters are mirror images of one another.

Mohawk: A turn from forward to back or back to forward and from one foot to the other foot of the same edge while changing directions.

Olympian: One who has performed in the Olympics.

Open hip: A position in which the free leg is partially turned against the hip joint.

Pair skating: A team of two skaters who do daring jumps and lifts.

Pinwheel: (1) A partner move of two skaters both in a modest spread-eagle position. (2) In synchronized skating: a group of skaters in one line with half the skaters facing the opposite direction of the other half.

Pom-poms: Something your grandmother wore on her skates to decorate the toe area. Not recommended: unsafe when doing crossovers.

Pop or **popping:** When the skater comes up in the skating knee too quickly.

Pops: As in a jump, when timing and position are badly off. Skater immediately pulls out for the landing exit, rather than trying to save the jump and have the full rotation.

Precision skating: Also called synchronized or ensemble skating. Usually made up of eight to twenty-four skaters.

Professional: An instructor of figure skating mostly for intermediate level students.

Program: Skating that is intended to match the music in sound and in spirit.

Progressive: An ice dance term of two or three steps done on a lobe.

PSA: Professional Skaters Association. An organization that promotes the betterment of teachers, instructors, professionals, and coaches. Their rating system sets standards for teaching this sport.

Quad: A jump of four or, if an axel, four-and-a-half revolutions in the air. Very difficult.

RFO: Right forward outside edge.

RFI: Right forward inside edge.

RBO: Right back outside edge.

RBI: Right back inside edge.

RFF: Right forward flat.

RBF: Right back flat.

Radius (of the blade): The curve of the blade from toe pick to heel. Usually from seven feet up to eight-and-a-half feet. Freestylists tend to choose seven-foot radii. Ice dances tend to choose seven-and-a-half or eight-foot radii.

Radius (of a circle): A measurement from the middle of the circle to the edge of the circle.

Railing: The barrier, or wall around the rink.

Reverse kilian position: An ice dance position where the woman is to the left of the man.

Roll: A tracing similar in shape to a half-circle. Also called a swing roll, or an edge.

Salchow: A jump invented by Ulrich Salchow (could have been called an Ulrich). One revolution in the air. Take-off is from a back inside edge.

Serious skater: One who skates just about every day.

Shadow skating: The tracings of two skaters are in line with one another.

Sharpening: Redefining the hollow, or concave part of the blade. Very basic guidelines are: for a beginner, one-half-inch hollow, for an intermediate, seven-sixteenths-inch hollow, and for a serious skater, three-eighths of an inch hollow sharpening (see p. 169).

Shoot-the-duck: A position balanced on one fully bent leg with the other leg extended in front.

Short program: The first part of single and pair competitions. It is two minutes and forty seconds in length, but it must include eight required moves. It accounts for one-third of the total mark.

Skate: The boot part of the skate that is laced and the attached metal blade.

Skating foot, skating arm, skating side, etc.: If the skater is balancing on the right foot, the right side of the body is called the skating side. Hence, the skating foot, skating arm, etc.

Slide: A fall.

Snowplow stop: A stop made by scraping one blade against the ice.

Soakies: A fabric covering for the protection of the blades and to absorb moisture.

Sponsor: Someone who helps a competitive skater financially.

Spread eagle: A freestyle move where both feet are facing opposite directions, one is going forward and the other is going backward.

Spiral: An old-fashioned term for an arabesque, a move on one foot, with the other foot extended back and higher than the head of the skater.

Stroking: Also called "skating." Pushing off against the inside edge of the blade you were last on. Never push from the toe pick.

Store-bought skates: Skates that are sized to fit your foot.

Surgeon's knot: A single knot followed by crossing the laces in opposite directions. Done near the top of the skate boot.

Sweet spot: The perfect spot on your blade for spinning. The first toe pick will graze, but not scrape, the ice surface.

Swing roll: A shape that is similar to a half-circle tracing. Also called a roll and an edge. It is done on one foot.

Swizzle: A lemon-shaped maneuver done on two feet forward or backward.

Synchronized skating: Also called ensemble or precision skating. Usually done by eight to twenty-four skaters.

"T" position: (A starting position.) The feet make a "T." One foot is turned out, with the heel placed at the instep of the other.

Teacher: An instructor of figure skating that starts beginners in basic moves.

Test: Meaning a physical achievement test, usually to qualify for competition.

Three turn: A turn made on one foot. The tracing looks like the number "3."

Thirty-three turn: A turn made on two feet. The tracing looks like the number "33."

Throw jump: When one skater throws his partner into a jump. Also called partner-assisted jump.

Toe pick: Those pointed picks at the front of your blade. Great for taking off and landing jumps and for balancing in a spin. But toe picks can cause a fall if you lean too far forward.

Tongue: The leather or fabric piece of your skate boot that covers the laces.

Tracing, tracings: The mark left on the ice by the skaters' blade.

Traveled spin: A spin that has tracings that start in one place and end in another. The opposite of traveled is a centered spin.

USFSA: The United States Figure Skating Association. The governing body of United States skaters who choose to take tests and enter competitions that can lead to World and Olympic events.

"V" position: (A starting position.) The feet make a "V." The heels of both feet are touching and the toes of each foot are pointing out.

Waltz jump: An early learning jump from forward to backward.

Wang, Vera: A clothing designer who also designs skating costumes.

Whaxel: A combination of the words "whoa" and "axel." It's a goof. The skater jumps off, intending to do an axel, but misses her timing by bringing her free foot forward too soon, then yells, "Whoa" as she pops the jump. Looks scary and feels awful.

Wheelbarrow: Two skaters in a move in which the front skater is in a shoot-the-duck position, and the back skater is in an arabesque.

Zamboni: The ice resurfacing machine that scrapes, lays water, and spreads the water to freeze and make new, or "clean" ice.

RESOURCES

Recommended Books, Videos, Web Sites, Magazines, and Organizations for Figure Skating

Books of instruction

Morrissey, Peter, and James Young. *Figure Skating School*. Buffalo, N.Y.: Firefly Books, 1997.

Petkevich, John Misha. *Sports Illustrated Figure Skating: Championship Techniques*. New York: Sports Illustrated, 1989.

Shulman, Carole, and Donald Laws. *The Complete Book of Figure Skating*. Champaign, Ill.: Human Kinetics, 2002.

Yamaguchi, Kristi. *Figure Skating for Dummies*. Foster City, Calif.: IDG Books, 1997.

Book for great photos and short biographies

Milton, Steve, and Geraud Chataigneau. *Figure Skating Now*. 2d ed. Buffalo, N.Y.: Firefly Books, 2003.

Photo essay for younger readers

Feldman, Jane. *I Love Skating!* New York: Random House Books for Young Readers, 2002.

Skating's greatest sourcebook for everything relating to figure skating

Berman, Alice. *Skater's Edge Sourcebook: Ice Skating Resource Guide*. 3rd ed. Kensington, Md.: The Skater's

Edge, 2003. Box 500, Kensington, MD 20895;
www.skatersedgemag.com; e-mail: skateredge@aol.com.

Figure skating magazine (with articles about the skating
stars, behind the scenes, and listings of upcoming
competitions)

International Figure Skating Magazine
44 Front Street, Suite 590
Worcester, MA 01608
tel: 508-756-2595
www.ifsmagazine.com/glg

Videos

About the stars/behind the scenes
Figure Skating Superstars: Katarina Witt and Friends
(available through www.skatersedgemag.com)

Instruction
BASICS! Eyeskate Foundations by Bobby and Barbie
    Martin (VHS)
(available through www.skatersedgemag.com)

Understanding figure skating competitions
Spectator's Guide to Figure Skating by Ann-Margreth
    Frei (VHS)
(available through www.skatersedgemag.com)

Web sites

www.kidsdomain.com/sports/iceskate
www.fogsonice.com/skateweb

For parents and kids

www.telusplanet.net/public/goodskat/

For skating fans

sk8stuff.com

Links where you can purchase your skating clothes and accessories:
capeziodance.com/catalog.html
www.rainbosportsshop.com
www.skatenwear.com

Skating organizations

The Ice Skating Institute: www.skateisi.org
The Professional Skaters Association: www.skatepsa.com
The United States Figure Skating Association:
   www.usfsa.org

INDEX

About the Author

RIKKI RENDICH SAMUELS has been involved in figure skating since she was five years old. As a USFSA national competitor, she received her gold medal in figures and free style. As a professional, she has been awarded the highest awards from the Professional Skaters Association, a master's rating in figures and freestyle, and a master's rating in program administration. Her articles have appeared in *Skater's Edge* and *Skating* magazine. For the past twenty years she has taught thousands of beginners and advanced skaters at The Rink at Rockefeller Center and at Sky Rink in New York City. She previously taught skating at West Point Military Academy. She lives on New York's Upper West Side and commutes to work by skating on inline skates.